THE FUN FACTS DICTIONARY

A World of Weird and Wonderful Words

Bernadette McCarver Snyder

LIGUORI
PUBLICATIONS

One Liguori Drive
Liguori, Missouri 63057-9999
(314) 464-2500

Imprimi Potest:
James Shea, C.SS.R.
Provincial, St. Louis Province
The Redemptorists

Imprimatur:
Monsignor Maurice F. Byrne
Vice Chancellor, Archdiocese of St. Louis

ISBN 0-89243-348-5
Library of Congress Catalog Card Number: 91-72204

Scripture selections taken from THE NEW AMERICAN BIBLE WITH
REVISED NEW TESTAMENT, copyright © 1986, by the Confrater-
nity of Christian Doctrine, Washington, DC, are used with per-
mission. All rights reserved.

Webster's New Universal Unabridged Dictionary, Deluxe
Second Edition, copyright © 1983, Simon and Schuster, Inc.,
used as a reference.

Cover and interior art by Chris Sharp

DEDICATION

I dedicate this dictionary to all my teachers —
especially my mother —
who taught me to look beyond ordinary definitions;
to peek around, under, and inside;
to give in to giggles and welcome wonderment;
to see the rainbow in a raindrop
and find a WOW in each fresh new day.

INTRODUCTION

The difference between the right word and ALMOST the right word is the difference between lightning and lightning bug.

Mark Twain

What IS a dictionary? It's a book where you can look up new words, old words, words you wonder about, words you've never heard about. The dictionary defines and describes WORDS.

What are "fun facts"? They're facts that might surprise or amaze you or make you giggle — facts that are FUN to discover!

So a fun facts dictionary is a combination of the two! You can use it to look up some serious words and some silly words. You can find out what words mean or where they came from or how people use them or misuse them.

You can discover an abelmosk and ambergris, the difference between calabash and columbine, the meaning of balneology and campanology, some little-known traditions and superstitions, inventions and interventions, originations and embarkations.

So are you ready to jump into a weird world of words? Ready to find out facts that only a few people have heard about? Ready to be surprised — and then surprise someone else with whatever surprised you? Ready to oh, aah, gawk, and giggle?

Then turn this page!

Start to look up right now. Looking DOWN makes you frown. Looking UP helps you stretch your neck AND your imagination. Whee! What word will you look up first?

 # IS FOR...

Aah

Aah is what a doctor tells you to say while he's sticking a stick down your throat. You might want to bite off the end of the stick but instead you're supposed to relax and say "aaaaah." Well, maybe relaxing will make your throat feel better. Maybe relaxing would make YOU feel better right now. Put your feet up. Put all your black clouds away. Start at the top of your head and move all the way to the tip of your toes, relaxing your ear muscles, your collarbone muscles, your elbow muscles, and your think muscles. And when you're all relaxed, really say AAH! Now you're ready for blue skies, white clouds, and clear sailing on a sea of discovery. Sail into the future, into the past, around to the other side of the world. And what will you use for a ship? Why, this book of course! This *Fun Facts Dictionary* can be the windjammer that sails you into the sea of surprises, the tugboat that pulls you up on the shores of silliness, the lifeboat that invites you to make your life more interesting by discovering the weird and wonderful world of words. Now say aah....

Aardwolf

Aardwolf is a four-legged animal found in southern and eastern Africa. You MAY have heard of an aardvark, which is an African anteater that is sometimes called an earth pig! Well, an aardwolf is more like a hyena, and it is sometimes called an earth wolf. Do you know anyone who eats like a pig or howls like a wolf? Sometimes it's "ard" to tell people from animals when they act greedy or make loud ugly noises and FORGET that people are supposed to have better manners than animals! Of course, YOU would never act like a pig or a wolf, would you? WOULD you?

Abecedarian

Abecedarian is someone who is either learning or teaching the ABC's! Do you know YOUR ABC's? Do you know how to alphabetize something or put something in alphabetical order? Did you know that, in alphabetical order, the word *abacus* comes BEFORE the word *abecedarian*? An abacus is a frame with sliding beads that people once used for counting — and in some parts of the world, some people STILL use an abacus to count because they don't have calculators. Can you believe that? NO calculators! BUT who needs a calculator to count your blessings! Have YOU counted your blessings today? Well, why don't you start counting right now?

Abelmosk

Abelmosk is a bushy herb of the mallow family. But DON'T look for it in the marshmallow section of the grocery store! Instead, invite your best friend to go with you on an abelmosk hunt! Go to the library and see if you can find a picture of an abelmosk. Then explore your neighborhood looking for one. You might NOT find one, but you WILL find lots of OTHER interesting bushes and things that God made. Wasn't it nice of God to "plant" strange and exciting things all over the world — just for YOU to discover?

Abhor

Abhor is an ugly-sounding word for an ugly kind of feeling. It means to hate or detest something. What do YOU abhor? It's okay to abhor something bad like sin, but never abhor a person. God made ALL people, so all people MUST have some good in them somewhere — even those who might be EASY to abhor! Remember that some people SEEM unlovable because they are unloved — or because they're sad or in pain or lonely or alone. Hate sin, but never hate sinners. Say a prayer for all sinners today.

Abracadabra

Abracadabra is a magic word! A magician will swirl his cape, twirl his mustache, and then wave his "magic wand" while he utters the magic word, "Abracadabra!" Magically, a plain glass of water turns into a glistening crystal prism, an ordinary white handkerchief becomes a fluffy white bunny rabbit, a green frog on a rock changes into a blue bird on a twig! Wow! Don't you wish YOU could work magic like that? Well, you can! Every time you look into the mirror and see a grouchy, gloomy face there, think of the funniest movie you ever saw or the funniest thing that ever happened to you. And then watch out! You just might abracadabra that grump into a grin! You MIGHT start to giggle, snicker, chortle, and snort. And then people will wonder what happened to YOU! Well, don't tell them. Just let this trick be your own abracadabra secret!

Absolution

Absolution means pardon or forgiveness for a sin or a mistake. Whenever you do something bad, hurry up and tell God you're sorry and you won't ever do it again. Ask God to give you absolution, forgiveness. You'll feel so much better after you talk to God about bad things that worry you. In fact, you'll feel better after you talk to God about ANY thing!

Acerbity

Acerbity refers to the sour taste you might get if you bit into a lemon — or a green persimmon. Did you ever eat a persimmon? If you ever bit into a green one, you would KNOW what acerbity means! Try to find a persimmon tree — or a store that sells persimmons — and eat a RIPE persimmon. You might like it. Or you might not. But it's always fun to try NEW tastes, new adventures, new ideas. It's safe and snug to always eat and do the same old things, but what if you just kept on drinking milk from a bottle like a baby and NEVER tried to eat anything else? Wow! You sure would have missed a lot of good things!

Adjutant

Adjutant is a word that means helper or assistant. In the United States Army there is a rank called an ADJUTANT GENERAL. But did you know this word can also mean a big stork? This kind of bird is usually found in India and is also called an ADJUTANT BIRD or an ADJUTANT CRANE. Would YOU be a good adjutant? Are you a good helper? If you're not, maybe you should start trying to be! Help somebody today and maybe some day you'll be an adjutant general (instead of just a big bird!).

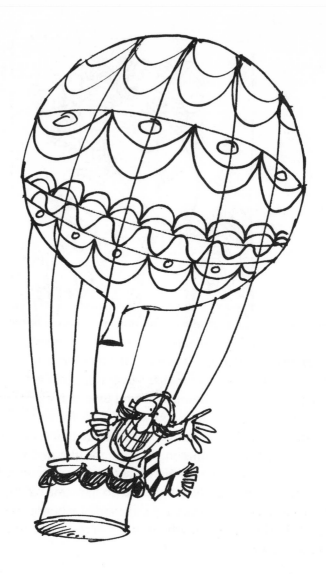

Aeronautics

Aeronautics is the science that has to do with operating an aircraft. Would you like to be the pilot of a spaceship or a hot-air balloon driver? Maybe you might like to study aeronautics or one of the other sciences. But if you don't, you can always use the science of your IMAGINATION! By using your mind and your imagination, you can travel anywhere, do anything, be anybody. Where will you fly today? What will you do? Who will you be? Just remember — it's okay to be "aery" but don't be "nauty."

Ambergris

Ambergris is a waxy substance that comes from whales, an oil that sometimes coats the nets of fishermen, a gooey something that has a greasy-sounding name. But what do you guess it's used for? You'll never believe it! It's not used to fry hamburgers or grease cars or soften baseball gloves. It's used to make perfume! Long ago, Arab fishermen noticed its sweet odor and discovered that it could be used in perfume as a "fixative" to make an aroma last longer. Soon ambergris was worth its weight in gold! Well, almost. It became VERY valuable. But today scientists have learned to make synthetic ambergris, so now whales don't have to worry about getting chased by perfume makers! What else do you know that is a synthetic — nylon, orlon, fake friends? YOU don't have any fake friends, do you? REAL friends may be hard to find — but they're worth the search.

Annoyance

Annoyance is what you cause when you do the wrong thing at the wrong time! It's fun to talk; but talking annoys others if you do it in the wrong place — like at a movie when OTHERS are trying to listen. It's fun to run — but it can bother others if you don't look where you're going and bump into someone! Has anyone ever been an annoyance to you? Have YOU ever been an annoyance to someone else? Think before you act — so you can do the right thing at the right time instead of the wrong thing at the wrong time!

Answer

Answer is the opposite of a question. But now, you KNEW that, didn't you? You ask a question, you get an answer. Well, sometimes you get one. Not always. Sometimes you ask and ask and nobody listens and nobody answers. And that makes you feel bad and sad, doesn't it? Well, how do you think other persons feel when they ask YOU a question and never get an answer? Maybe a friend or someone in your family asks you, "What did you do today?" or "Where are you going?" and you DON'T answer. Oh, oh. Somebody's gonna feel bad. Or maybe somebody asks you to help. Or to share. Or to take time for a hug. And you don't even bother to answer. Oh, oh. Somebody's gonna feel sad. Maybe today you should think about what kind of answers you've been giving. Maybe if you GAVE better answers, you'd GET better answers!

Ante Meridiem

Ante meridiem is not a word for somebody's aunt who is named Meridiem! It's a Latin term that means "before noon." That's why you call six o'clock in the morning six a.m. — or you might call it way too early to expect anybody to wake up and get ready to go somewhere! Another Latin term is *post meridiem* and that means "after noon," so you would call three o'clock in the afternoon three p.m. — or you might call it time for a snack, yum-yum! Do you know any other Latin terms or words? Well, there's "Adeste Fideles," the Christmas song that is also called "O Come, All Ye Faithful" and *e pluribus unum,* which means "out of many, one" and is the motto of the U.S.A. And then there's *Deo gratias,* which means "thanks to God." Aren't you THANKFUL that you don't have to speak in Latin? What other Latin words can you learn today?

Automatic

Automatic is a word that usually refers to something done by machinery, without YOUR working on it. An automatic automobile shifts gears so you don't have to. An automatic telephone-answering machine takes messages for you when you're not at home. Wouldn't it be great if there was a way to get homework and chores done automatically? Well, maybe not. When something or someone does your work for you, then YOU never learn how to do it yourself! If you only knew how to count by using a calculator, you wouldn't even know how to count out change to buy a hamburger without using your calculator! If you got somebody else to laugh for you, you wouldn't have much fun. When you DO things for yourself, you learn. So what will you do to learn something new today?

 # IS FOR...

Bagatelle

Bagatelle is a trifle, a little thing of no importance. Of course, sometimes people disagree about a bagatelle. Some people think a pretty marble or a crayon drawing or the first star of the night or the last jellybean in the jar are bagatelles. Others think they are treasures. Some people think it is a little thing of no importance when they promise to do something with you or for you — and then don't bother to do it. YOU might think this is NOT a trifling matter. You might get your feelings hurt or decide to never, never trust that person again. Or maybe YOU might not bother to keep a promise and somebody ELSE might get hurt feelings. Think about the BAGATELLES in your life today. What do YOU think is a trifle or a treasure? When do you get hurt? When do you hurt someone else? And why?

Bairnteam

Bairnteam is a funny word. What do you guess it means? A barn for a baseball team? Nope, it's an old Scottish word that means CHILDREN! Yep! BAIRN means a child and BAIRNTEAM means children! Wouldn't it be great if bairnteam always had "TEAM SPIRIT" — playing together to have fun, working together to achieve a goal, instead of complaining and whining about one another or fighting or causing trouble? What do YOU think adults should do to help today's bairnteam play and work together more happily? Talk about this with someone today.

Balaustine

Balaustine is the name of a wild pomegranate tree. But what's a pomegranate? And do you know what it has to do with Christianity? Well, a pomegranate is about the size of an orange, and it has a thick red skin and is full of lots and lots of seeds. When it gets really, really ripe — or mature — on the tree, it bursts and the seeds go in all directions. The design of a pomegranate was used in the wood-carvings and decorations of many early Christian churches because it seemed to be a good "symbol" for Christianity — a lot of people all together in one "skin," just "bursting" with the "Good News," ready to go in all directions to spread the "seeds" of faith. What could YOU do to spread Christianity? What do you think faith means? Think about that today.

Balloon

Balloon is an airtight bag filled with hot air. Does that mean a person who is full of "hot air" is a balloon? Not really. But you might find that kind of person where there ARE balloons — at birthday parties, parades, or other kinds of celebrations. But wait a minute — there are lots of different meanings for this word. In chemistry, a balloon is a round vessel with a short neck; in architecture, it's a ball or a globe on the top of a pillar; in weaving, it's a reel on which yarn is wound. And do you know what it is in a cartoon? Yep, it's an outline that encloses the words said by the cartoon character. Why don't you draw a cartoon today of YOURSELF — and draw a balloon over your head with the kind of words you use when you talk like you are full of "hot air"!

Balneology

Balneology is the science of bathing. I bet you didn't know taking a bath was SCIENCE! Well, actually this means the kind of bathing that is therapeutic — the kind used to help heal or soothe someone. Suppose you sprained a muscle — the doctor might tell you to spend some time in a nice warm bath to soothe the muscle and help it heal. Or suppose a football player got injured in a game and had to have surgery on a knee or elbow — afterward he might have to soak the knee or elbow in a "whirlpool" kind of bath to help it heal. Surprise someone today by saying you're going to immerse yourself in balneology!

Basenji

Basenji is a "barkless" dog that CAN make a howling sound but seldom does. There is also a New Guinea "singing" dog that sometimes makes a melodic yodeling sound. But MOST dogs are the barking kind. People who study animals report observing one dog that barked continually for SEVEN hours and a cocker spaniel that barked 907 times in just ten minutes. That's a lot of barking! Do you ever get up in the morning and feel like "barking" at everybody you meet? Nobody seems to know why some days start out right and you feel like singing and other mornings make you feel like growling and grumbling. The next time you have "one of those days," why don't you PRETEND you're a Basenji — and keep your bark to yourself!

Bat

Bat can be a stick or club which is used to hit a ball OR it can be a little flying animal that sometimes lives in caves and is often pictured as a scary creature at Halloween. Some people think flying bats are really weird; but in China these little winged mammals are thought of as messengers of good luck. In fact, the Chinese symbols for "bat" and for "good luck" are very similar, and both words are pronounced as "fu." So if you were in China, you might hear someone say, "Look! Up in the air. Is it a bird? Is it a bat? No, it's a good luck!" You probably WOULDN'T hear someone say that — but you might! Well, that's just another example of how you can't judge a book by its cover or a bat by its reputation. Always look for the GOOD in life and make your OWN good luck!

Battery

What happens when the battery "goes dead" in your watch, your radio, your camera, or your flashlight? No time, no music, no photographs, no light! So be thankful for a man named Alessandro Volta, a physics professor who invented the first electric battery in 1800. Since then, scientists have developed all kinds of batteries, so today they come in all kinds of shapes and sizes — to give power to all kinds of things that YOU see! And did you know that electrical power is measured in units called "volts" in honor of the professor who invented the battery? Did you ever LOOK at a battery? It doesn't LOOK like much, does it? But what happens when you have a flashlight but NO batteries? What else can you think of that doesn't LOOK like much but makes a BIG difference in the world?

Benefactor

Benefactor is a helper — someone who gives money or some kind of benefit to others who need it. One famous benefactor was a man named Andrew Carnegie. He came from a very poor family and had to go to work in a factory when he was just a little boy. By the time he was thirteen, he was given complete charge of a big steam engine. When he was fifteen, he began delivering telegrams and learned the telegraph code and system so well that he soon became superintendent of the agency! With luck and hard work he eventually became one of the richest men in America. And what do you guess he did with all his money? Well, Carnegie believed that you should USE money to be a benefactor — to help make the community better and to help people help themselves. So Carnegie gave hundreds of MILLIONS of dollars to build libraries, schools, and museums all across America. In fact, they say that for every twenty dollars Carnegie ever made, he GAVE AWAY nineteen dollars! Would you do that? Would you give away nineteen dollars and keep only one dollar for yourself? Think about what would happen if EVERYBODY was as generous as Carnegie. What a difference that would make in the world!

Blue Moon

Blue moon is a term people use when they talk about something that only happens once in a while. Do you know why? And did you ever see a blue moon? Maybe you did and didn't know it! When you see a "new" moon, it is just a sliver of a semicircle in the sky, but then it changes each night until you see a "full" moon, or a complete circle. A full moon shows up every twenty-nine and a half days, so you usually see only ONE full moon in one month; BUT about every thirty-two months, you can see TWO full moons in one month and this is known as a "blue" moon. When the weather conditions are right, the moon can appear to be blue in color. Since you have to wait almost three years between each blue moon, people use the term "once in a blue moon" to describe something that takes a long time to happen. Did you ever have to wait a long time for something you wanted to happen or to get or to achieve? Are you waiting for something right now? Are you wishing someone would give you a gift? Well, why don't you save your money and earn it! Are you wishing to have a special career some day? Study and work hard and BELIEVE you can do it! Don't get discouraged. Anything that is worthwhile is worth waiting for. But you probably won't get it if you just WAIT. Work while you wait, whistle while you work!

Buzzworm

Buzzworm is an old southwestern term for rattlesnake. When a rattlesnake buzzes, you better buzz off! Did you know there is an unusual flower, a type of orchid, that is named "rattlesnake plan-tain"? And did you know some people are known as "rattlebrains" because they seem to be empty-headed and talk a lot about nothing? Did you ever see a rattlebrain buzzing around, using buzz-words (slang words that are "in" for the moment)? Well, don't YOU be a buzzworm OR a rattlebrain. Don't speak before you think. Think before you speak.

C IS FOR...

Caboodle

Caboodle means a group or a bunch of things — so you might refer to all your STUFF as the whole "caboodle." This word is a combination of kit and boodle, which means family (kit) and possessions (boodle). Today, some people seem to forget to put their kit before their boodle! THINGS are nice to have — a warm bed to sleep in, comfortable shoes to run in, a VCR to watch movies with, a new baseball glove to play ball with. But you COULD live without them! PEOPLE are more important. Like everyone, you need family or friends — someone to laugh at your jokes or give you a hug or "kiss it and make it well," someone you care about and who cares about you. Do you spend too much time worrying about how to get more boodle? Should you spend MORE time telling God thanks for your kit, doing nice things that will make a hit with your kit, showing your kit you care? Use your noodle — put your kit before your boodle!

Caboose

Caboose comes last. It's the name for that jazzy-looking little car that usually trails along at the end of a train. It might be fun to ride in the last car on a train, but it usually is NOT fun to BE last — to be chosen last for a team, to come in last in a race, to be thought of as the last or the loser. But, then, who cares? If you're last chosen, at least you're on the team. If you come in last but tried your best, you're still a champion. Never worry about whether you're the caboose at the end OR the chug-chug engine at the front. Wherever you are, make the most of it and ENJOY the trip!

Cacophony

Cacophony is a harsh, jarring sound. Some grownups think rock music is a cacophony. Some children think grownups arguing or fussing make the worst cacophony. Would YOU ever make trouble by causing a cacophony? Today, try just the opposite. Discover silence. Find a very quiet spot and just sit there for a long time, all by yourself. Immerse yourself in the silence the way you might immerse yourself in the shallow end of a nice cool swimming pool on a hot day. Relax. Listen. Be cool. Maybe you'll hear little sounds you never heard before. Maybe you'll think thoughts you never thought before. Maybe you'll even hear God talking to you, telling you something important, telling you that you are special — and loved.

Calabash

Calabash sounds like it could mean a big party or bash held in a "calaboose" — which is another name for a jail! Actually, a calabash is a gourd — the hard-skinned fruit of a tropical tree. The calabash gourd has a skin so hard it can be used to make a bowl or a pipe or a bottle! Did you ever know a PERSON who was "hard-skinned" — hard to hurt but also hard to get to know? Sometimes people become hard-skinned to PROTECT themselves. They won't let anybody or anything bother them because they're AFRAID to get hurt. But that's a lonely way to live. If you know people like that, try to "get under their skin"! Try to make friends — because hard-skinned people usually NEED friends.

Camel

Camel is an animal that is one of the world's most astonishing creatures. Someone once joked that a "camel is a horse put together by a committee" because it seems like a strange assortment of mismatched parts. Actually, the one-humped Arabian camel is a masterpiece of nature. It can travel for miles without water and survive the savage sun and scorching winds of the desert! It has its own "sunglasses" — thick bushy eyebrows and long eyelashes — that protect its eyes from the blowing desert sand. For short distances it can carry up to one thousands pounds — MORE than an elephant! And it will eat almost ANYTHING, including its owner's tent! Mark Twain once said, "I expect it would be a real treat to a camel to have a keg of nails for dinner." Unfortunately, camels are also

stubborn, sullen, bad-tempered, and easily offended. When they get mad at a camel driver, they often "get even" by biting, spitting, or trampling on his feet. Do you know any PEOPLE who act like that? Hmmm...if you DO, maybe you should serve them a keg of nails for dinner! Or better yet, maybe you should TREAT THEM VERY NICE and SHOW them that it's better to NOT behave like a camel!

Campanology

Campanology could have something to do with camping — but it doesn't. This word means the art of ringing bells! Did you know ringing a bell could be an art? Did you ever hear bells rung in a musical way? Did you ever watch someone pulling on the big long rope that rings a huge bell in a bell tower? Did you ever hear the bell on an ice-cream truck? Now, THAT'S the BEST kind of campanology in the summertime! Ring the bell today by doing something exciting! Maybe you could do a chore BEFORE somebody forces you to do it. OR maybe you could write a poem, sing a song, or LOOK for something special God might want you to see! Or maybe you could eat an ice-cream cone or a Popsicle and say a little prayer to thank God for the happy ding-a-ling of bells and the delicious drip-drip of ice cream.

Cash Register

Cash register is a money machine that can look old-fashioned and make a ringing sound each time it rings up a sale — or it can look as mod as a spaceship and work like a computer. The first cash register was invented by James J. Ritty in 1879. How many years was that BEFORE you were born? Maybe YOU would like to be an inventor like Mr. Ritty. What would you like to invent? Cash in on today by doing some daydreaming about all the inventions that have been "thought up" by someone SINCE you were born — and then think up an invention of your own!

Columbine

Columbine is a plant with delicate foliage and unusual "spurred" blossoms that are bright and beautiful — and it is a member of the crowfoot family. Now you wouldn't think a flower that was the member of the crowfoot family could be very much, would you? You might think its blossoms would be as ugly as a crow's foot! But you can never judge a flower — OR a person — by the family tree! People can't choose their families — but they CAN choose their friends! So be careful how you choose YOUR friends. Look beyond the family, beyond the beauty. Someone whose family IS as ugly as a crow's foot COULD BE a beautiful flower, a special person, a wonderful friend.

Clock

Clock is an instrument for measuring time and then showing you what time it is — so you'll know whether you're early or late or just in time for dinner! At first, the only way people measured time was by sunrise and sunset. They got up when it got light and worked until it got dark. Then people began to invent interesting things — the sundial, the hourglass, the windup clock, the electric clock, AND the wrist watch — so you could have time on your hands! How do you measure YOUR time? By how much work you get done? By how many things you learn? By how much fun you have? Time is precious. Measure it well. Spend it wisely.

 **IS FOR...**

Derring-do

Derring-do is a way to describe someone who dares to do! However, this term is usually used for someone who chooses "to do" in a reckless or dashing fashion — like the movie pirate who brandishes a sword as he leaps from the deck of one ship to another or a cop who leaps from rooftop to rooftop to catch a criminal. Derring-do can be exciting in a movie, but it can be dangerous in real life! So always dare to do — to adventure, to explore, and to learn — but be smart enough to also dare to be cautious. Say a prayer today to ask God to protect and guide you in all you DO!

Desperado

Desperado sounds exciting, but it actually describes a desperate outlaw. Have you ever been desperate — like maybe desperate to get a candy bar? Have you ever been an outlaw — like maybe knowing the family rules but breaking them anyway? Some people might think a desperado like Jesse James lived an exciting life; but he was probably lonely and scared, always running away because he had broken the law. It's sometimes HARD to obey the laws, but it's a lot better than feeling like an outlaw!

Dibble

Dibble is a pointed tool which you use to dig holes in the ground so you can plant seeds, young plants, or bulbs. No, not light bulbs — flower bulbs! MAYBE if you planted a light bulb, a lamp would grow but probably NOT. But if you planted a tulip bulb, a pretty flower would grow. Bulbs are really big seeds and at one time certain types of tulip bulbs were so special, they cost thousands of dollars apiece! Today, they are much less expensive, and you can see tulips growing in gardens in many parts of the world. Of course, you don't HAVE to use a dibble to plant them. You CAN use a shovel — or even an old tablespoon. Why don't you plant some bulbs or seeds today — either in a garden or in a flowerpot in the kitchen. It's always fun to watch things grow — things like plants, babies, and ideas!

Dog

Dog is a four-legged animal that can be your best friend, likes to bark and eat, and usually has a very waggly tail. Suppose you had a dog named Rover. He would get so excited and happy to see you that he would almost look like he was smiling. He might like to curl up next to you when you are watching TV or even sleep by your bed at night. You would like him so much, you might start to think of him as part of the family — almost human. But dog experts say that Rover would probably think YOU are a DOG who has taken him into your den! Isn't that funny? Did you ever know that dogs probably think people are just tall dogs? The experts say a dog likes to stay close to his owner because he thinks of the owner as the "leader of the pack"! But dogs also expect the leader to provide food and protection — so when you "adopt" a dog, you become RESPONSIBLE for him. Of course, everybody in a family should be responsible and take care of everybody else. That's why it's so nice to be part of a family! Do you always remember to do YOUR part and SHARE in the care of the rest of YOUR family?

Dolphin

Dolphin is an intelligent, friendly sea creature that seems to LIKE people! In fact, dolphins have even rescued people! Dolphins live in groups or "families" called pods and use "echo location" — which means they use sound to find their food. They can often be seen leaping from the water high into the air, almost as though they were playing and having fun. There have been many eyewitness reports of dolphins rescuing people by keeping them afloat and saving them from drowning after boating accidents. Wouldn't it be fun to "play" with a dolphin? And don't you wish you could use SOUND to find food? Well, you CAN sometimes. When a friend is rattling a bag of potato chips, all you have to do is follow the sound to find the food! Why don't you get a book about dolphins from the library — and read it while you pretend to be a dolphin that has just "rescued" a bag of potato chips!

Dynamite

Dynamite was a bang-up idea invented by Alfred Nobel in 1867. He probably thought it would be a very helpful thing for the world because you could use it to clear the way to build new roads or buildings. For example, you could blast out a big rock that was too big to dig out. But some people used it to DESTROY things and to hurt other people. Maybe Nobel felt bad about that. Maybe that's why he established the famous NOBEL PRIZE. This is an important award that is given each year to people who have done something "distinguished" by working in the fields of chemistry, economics, physics, medicine, literature, or physiology. A special Nobel prize is given to the person who has done the most each year to try to promote world peace. Would YOU like to win the Nobel prize some year? Why don't you do some detective work and get information about each of the fields in which a Nobel prize is awarded? Maybe you might like to have a career in one of them. OR maybe you might like to work for world peace. You could BEGIN today by being "peaceful" with everybody you MEET — at home or away, in church, a store, or on your street. To bring peace to the world, you have to start with your OWN world!

 **IS FOR...**

Earmark

Earmark does NOT mean something ridiculous — like having a banana sticking out of your ear! Instead, it's a mark of identification or distinction. It sounds like a funny way to identify something, but it was first used when the EARS of cattle were MARKED by their owner's special mark, so if the animals got out and roamed the range, the cattlemen could identify which ones were whose property. Today, this term is used for other forms of identification OR to indicate something that has been set apart — for instance, when a mother says, "DON'T TOUCH those cookies — they're earmarked for the bake sale!" What is YOUR special earmark? Do you have a special way of talking, walking, laughing, combing your hair, or curling your lip? Maybe you have a special way of helping, noticing, listening, or cheering up! Think today about YOUR earmark and how you can USE it — OR maybe change it — to make God's world a little better.

Eccentric

Eccentric describes something that is irregular, off the center, out of the ordinary. Do you know anyone or anything that is eccentric? Some people thought Jesus was eccentric! He didn't do things in the ordinary way. He told people to "love their enemies." What? Instead of hating them? He said that if someone hurts you, you should "turn the other cheek." What? Instead of hitting back? He said to "love your neighbor as yourself." What? Instead of putting up a fence so your neighbor can't get near you? Some of the things Jesus taught certainly WERE and ARE eccentric, irregular — and wonderful. But now wait a minute. Think about that last one. How can you love your neighbor when you DON'T love yourself? Maybe there are some things about you that you don't LIKE. Maybe there are even some things about you that COULD be improved. But you ARE special. You ARE loved by God. And you should appreciate what you are and be thankful for your GOOD qualities, even when you're busy trying to improve the less-than-good ones. THEN, when you love yourself, it will be easier to love your neighbors, your friends, and your family too — the way eccentric Jesus taught everyone to do!

Ecclesiastical

Ecclesiastical is a fancy-sounding word that is sometimes used to describe *church* things. It comes from a Greek word which meant a gathering or assembly — and that's what a REAL church is! It's not just a building but the gathering of people who come together to pray and praise. The next time you go to church, you can tell all your friends you're doing something ecclesiastical!

33

Eke

Eke is a short word that has lots of meanings. It CAN mean to increase or prolong. It can mean to live very frugally with very little money. It can mean to add something that is missing — like when someone "ekes out" a living by working at a second job. Most people who have to eke out a living often say, "eek!" wondering if they are going to get all the bills paid each month. Some get very discouraged about being frugal, but OTHERS find it a challenge! They figure out ways to do more with less, to take advantage of every opportunity, and to ENJOY living even without much money! It's all a matter of ATTITUDE. What kind of attitude do YOU have? When you have to do something hard, do you say "eek" and give up? Or do you think of it as a challenge and find a way to "eke out" a solution? Pray for God to help you always have an attitude of gratitude!

Elaps

The word *elapse* means to glide or slide away or pass by — so you could say "two years have ELAPSED since we moved into this house." But the word *elaps* is the name for a certain kind of very poisonous SNAKE! (See what a difference adding an "e" to a word can make?) Have you ever heard of a coral snake? Well, that's one of the elaps species of snake. Did you ever think about the fact that a snake has no EARS? So how does it hear? Well, a snake's tongue is extremely sensitive to sound vibrations so by constantly flicking its tongue, the snake can pick up sound waves. This means you could say that a snake hears with its tongue! And here YOU thought a snake just liked to stick its tongue out at people! Do YOU ever stick your tongue out at people? If you do, you might HEAR them say something back that you WON'T like! Use your EARS today to listen to the sounds around you — to music, to giggles, to people talking — and be GRATEFUL for God's wonderful gift of SOUND!

THERE'S NO "E" ON ME.

Elephant

Of course, you know what an elephant is — but did you know an elephant can't jump? Elephants have the SAME kind of bones in their feet as other animals do, but elephant foot bones are packed closer together, so they DON'T have the same kind of "spring" mechanism that helps

other animals jump. It's probably a good thing! Can you imagine what it would be like if you were at a circus and a lot of huge elephants started jumping up and down? It would feel like an earthquake! Aren't you glad YOU can jump? Do some jumping today! Go outside and jump up and down and all around and tell God thanks for YOUR special "spring" mechanism!

Elevator

Elevator is a contraption that can raise or lift people or things up or down. The first elevator for people was invented by Elisha Graves Otis in 1857. Fifteen years later William Le Baron Jenney designed the first skyscraper — a ten-story building. Do you know why no one had ever built a skyscraper before? Well, why would they build a ten-story building when no one had invented an elevator yet? Who would want to climb ten flights of stairs? Sometimes one good invention triggers another! Today, there are much taller buildings all over the world. Some are over one hundred stories high. And they ALL have elevators! Some days when you're feeling really looooow, don't you wish somebody would invent an elevator that could raise or lift your spirits and make you feel like singing and dancing and flying to the moon? The only one who can invent that is YOU. When you get down, go ahead and let yourself feel really baaaaad for a little while and then push the UP button. Say a little prayer, sing a little song, or take a little walk and become your OWN elevator. Think about all the HAPPY things in your life and then raise up your head and shout, "GOING UP!" And then GO!

English

English is a language spoken by more than three hundred and fifty million people in the world! It is an important — and confusing — language. Suppose you were trying to teach other persons to speak English and you told them about the words *hear* (something you do with your ears) and *here* (where you ARE right now) but then explained that both words SOUND alike but are spelled differently and have different meanings. That would be confusing! And THEN you'd have to tell them about seen and scene, mean and mien, red and read, peer and pier, dear and deer. Oh, dear! See how confusing English could be if you didn't already know how to speak it? Sometimes it's confusing even if you DO know how to speak it — you say something nice but someone misunderstands and thinks you MEANT something not nice. But it's even worse if you DID mean to say something not nice. Be careful to never use hurtful words. Use healing words today — because tomorrow you may have to "eat your words."

Exercise

Exercise is something you do when you want to make your muscles strong enough to put some hop, skip, and jump into your life instead of flop, drop, and slump. There are only two things you HAVE to do to live an ordinary life. You have to eat and sleep. BUT if you want to be healthy and physically fit, you also have to get SOME exercise. Health experts say that if you get enough exercise, you won't have so many aches and pains and won't be so likely to feel sluggish, depressed, or BORED. Did you know SOME people only exercise their FINGERS — pushing buttons to play computer games or changing from one TV channel to another! Today, why don't you go outside and exercise your lungs by drinking in some fresh air, exercise your legs by taking a walk, exercise your eyes by looking around at all the wonders of the world, exercise your mind by thinking of all the GOOD things God has given you. Wow! Don't you feel better already?

IS FOR...

Far-flung

Far-flung is a word usually used to describe something far away —
even farther away than you could FLING it! You might say you are
going to explore far-flung places, meaning countries in another part
of the world. You might say you have far-flung friends, meaning
you know people who live in cities far away from the one where
you live. You might say you have far-flung ambitions or wishes.
OR you might say you wish somebody you don't like would get
flung far away! But of course, you would NEVER say that, would
you? Instead, you COULD say that you have one far-flung friend
who is always near — your friend God!

WOW! YOU FLUNG THAT!

Farkleberry

Farkleberry is a small bush or tree that has large white flowers and
round noneatable black berries. If friends of yours told you they had
a farkleberry bush in their yard, you might think they made up that
name — but it's a REAL bush. Sometimes jokes people make up
aren't as funny as the things that happen in real life. And yet SOME
people never seem to see ANYthing funny. To them, everything is
bleak and blah, doom and gloom. Don't ever let them get you down.
Life CAN be fun — if you let it be!

Farmer

Farmer is the name for someone who grows things. A farmer plants seeds in the ground and waits…then weeds, hoes, cultivates, watches the weather, and waits. A farmer must work hard and be patient, waiting for the seeds to sprout, grow, and turn into bushels of bright red ripe tomatoes, yellow squash, green cucumbers, and all the other different-colored, different-tasting things that start out as a tiny seed and turn into delicious food. ONE farmer wasn't satisfied to just wait and watch. He decided to experiment and turn farming into a "science." His name was Luther Burbank, and he was interested in nature when he was just a little boy. When he grew up, he tried new ways to grow flowers, fruits, and vegetables. You might say he was "busy as a bee" because bees take the pollen from one plant to the next — and Burbank did too. He experimented by "cross-pollinating" two different plants to make a NEW one! He developed many new kinds of plants, including the Burbank potato, the Shasta daisy, and a WHITE blackberry. He became a famous farmer and one of America's scientific heroes. There are ALL KINDS of heroes, you know — not just movie stars or sports stars. If YOU could be a hero, what KIND of hero would you like to be? Some ordinary people are heroes because, no matter what happens, they never give up. They always try to do the best they can. They live good lives and take good care of their families and love God and make the MOST of every new day, every new opportunity. Maybe they're the most important heroes of all!

Feathered Friends

Feathered friends is a term often used to describe birds. "Fine-feathered friends" is a term sometimes used to describe people who dress fancy. "Birds of a feather" usually means people or things that are a lot ALIKE. And you get a "feather in your cap" when you win an honor or an award. Did you know one of the finest feathered birds is the American BALD EAGLE — but it isn't bald! So WHY is it named that? Well, no one really knows but here's a guess. This eagle has plenty of feathers on its head, but the feathers are WHITE. So when seen from a distance, the bird's white feathers made it seem

that it was bald. People then called it a "bald" eagle; and the name stuck! Did you ever give someone a funny nickname — and then it stuck? Think of all the funny nicknames you've ever heard — but DON'T start calling your friends funny names or you might have FEWER friends tomorrow than you do today!

Flashlight

Flashlight is a light that you can carry with you and is usually operated by a small battery. It was first introduced over a hundred years ago by England's Bristol Electric Lamp Company, and it has been a good friend ever since to Boy Scouts, Girl Scouts, campers, and scaredy-cats of all ages and sizes. When all the electricity goes out, it's nice to have a flashlight by your side or in your hand so you can switch it on and turn off the dark! Anybody can turn into a scaredy-cat when things get dark. But did you ever think about the fact that you have another kind of flashlight that you can have ALWAYS with you? Sure! It's the light of God's love and protection. Whenever things get dark and you feel scared (even if it's in the middle of a sunny day), you can always say a prayer and let God's light shine in to brighten your outlook and warm up your insides. Isn't that a bright idea? Isn't it great to know you have your own personal flashlight — a light that doesn't even need batteries!

Flea

Flea is a tiny little insect that has gone to the dogs! Yep, fleas DO like to make their homes on dogs' backs. But did you know there are SNOW FLEAS that live way high in the Himalayan Mountains where it gets so cold that they freeze SOLID each night when the temperature drops drastically — and then they thaw out the next day? Can you imagine a flea ice cube thawing out and running off across the mountain? Well, if you think frozen fleas sound funny, what about a floating armadillo? Did you know that when an armadillo wants to cross a river, he gulps air until his stomach is full and then he slides into the water and floats across like a balloon? Aren't there a lot of strange insects and animals in the world? Aren't there a lot of strange HUMAN animals? Which one do you think is the most interesting insect? Which one do you think is the silliest animal?

Flivver

Flivver is a slang word for a small cheap automobile or airplane. Since small inexpensive contraptions like this often shake, rattle, and roll, you might begin to quiver when you ride in a flivver! Do you ever shake or shudder when you get scared? Most people DO! Even puppies shake when they're scared or excited. So the next time you're in a flivver, buckle up your safety belt and hang on tight! Then you won't need to quiver! When you're careful and look where you're going, flivvers can be fun — and life can be too!

Foreign

Foreign is something that is different from what YOU think of as ordinary. It could be a way of acting or talking that is ordinary to people in a country or a town or a neighborhood that is not YOUR country or town or neighborhood. For example, people in China often read books from back to front instead of from front to back. And they put footnotes at the TOP of the page instead of at the bottom. In ancient China there were many customs YOU might find strange. When a man met a friend, he shook his OWN hand instead of the friend's hand. When a woman served tea, she put the saucer OVER the cup (to keep it warm) instead of UNDER the cup to catch spills. And after taking a bath, people dried themselves with a WET towel! These customs may sound foreign to you, but to the Chinese they were ordinary. It's interesting for Americans to hear about the foreign customs of other countries. It's interesting for people from other countries to hear about the foreign customs of Americans. In God's family there are NO foreigners because ALL are brothers and sisters!

Frog

Frog is a grown-up tadpole! There are bullfrogs, leopard frogs, and even tree frogs. Frogs leap and sleep and can usually be found near water. But SOMETIMES you can get a frog in your throat! When people get sore throats and their voices sound husky and funny, they often say, "I've got a frog in my throat." Do you know WHY people say that? Well, way back in the Middle Ages when not much was known about medicine, if a person got a throat infection, the doctors would sometimes put a LIVE FROG, head first, into the patient's mouth! They thought the frog would inhale and breathe the infection INTO itself and OUT of the patient. Ever since, people have been using the expression "a frog in my throat" to describe throat problems. And that certainly WOULD be a problem — having a real frog in your mouth! Aren't you glad doctors use a DIFFERENT treatment for sore throats today? Frogs are probably glad too! Say a prayer today for doctors and for scientists who are working to make great LEAPS in medical discoveries.

Future

Future is something that hasn't come yet. It's tomorrow, some day, later. Are you always WAITING for the future? When someone asks you to do something, do you say, "I'll do it later"? When you have a dream or a goal, do you just wait for it to happen SOME day? Do you think waiting will get a chore done or make a dream come true? If you want a happy future, you have to start working toward it TODAY — studying, planning, and praying. What are your dreams for tomorrow, some day, later? What do you think you might DO NOW to start to make those dreams come true?

 **IS FOR...**

Galaxy

Galaxy is a grouping of millions of stars. OR this word is sometimes used to describe a gathering of human "stars" — people who are brilliant or famous, well known for some kind of work or achievement. Do YOU know any famous people? How about your family, your teachers, your friends? They may not be famous to the REST of the world, but they're well known to YOU! You see their work and "achievements" every day. Do you ever think to compliment them on the good work they do? Maybe this would be a good day to start. Make someone feel like a star today!

Gazebo

Gazebo is a "summerhouse" or a little structure in the yard where you can go and sit and enjoy the breeze and "gaze" at the garden or the sky or the world around you. Doesn't that sound like a nice thing to do on a summer day — or on ANY day? If it doesn't, then you must be TOO busy. It's always good to find time to sit for a while alone and GAZE, to do nothing but soak in the beauty of the day, to think happy thoughts, to hum a tune, to let God talk to YOU. Most people find time to PRAY, to talk TO God — but do you ever take time to be quiet and let God talk to YOU? He may have been calling and trying to get in touch with you, but the line was so busy, he could never get his call through! If you don't have your own gazebo (not many people do!), find SOME quiet spot to sit today for just a few minutes — to stop, look, and listen. You might enjoy it so much, you'll want to make it a habit — and start to gaze every day!

Gift

Gift is something given — to celebrate an occasion or simply as a thoughtful gesture. A gift could be a birthday present, a donation to the poor or to a worthy cause, or a gesture to say "I like you" or "Thank you" or "Surprise!" Did you ever get a special gift — on a special occasion OR as a surprise on an ordinary day? Did you ever think about the fact that God gave everyone the GIFT of life? And then he gave each person other gifts too — beauty, goodness, cheerfulness, imagination, a lovely voice, the ability to play sports well, a creative talent for art or writing or building or helping. What special gift did God give you? Think now. You might think you don't have ANY gifts, but you DO. God gave EVERY person a gift OR gifts. Decide what your BEST gift is. Decide how you can best use it.

Giggle

Giggle is a silly laugh that can be a lot of fun. OR it can get you in trouble if you giggle at the wrong time — like right in the middle of something SERIOUS. Maybe you have the gift of giggle! It's important to be serious about some things in life, but it's also important to be able to RECOGNIZE the funny things in life, to watch for the giggles hidden in with the worries. And one of the BEST gifts is to be able to laugh at yourself! The next time you get embarrassed about something or feel self-conscious or worried about doing just the right thing at just the right time, try to find something happy or hopeful in the situation and then allow yourself a quiet giggle. It will make you feel better. And it might make others feel better too!

Gloss

Gloss is a shine, a brightness, a luster. What can you think of that looks glossy — a shoe that's been shined, an icicle in the sunshine, a shirt made of silk? What else? Did you know there's another word that's similar but different? That word is GLOSSARY. You will often find a glossary at the back of a book. It adds notes or explanations about information in the book — so you might say a glossary puts a shine on words! What could you do to put a shine on today? Water the flowers? Clean up a room and use furniture polish to shine up a table and chairs? Open the blinds or curtains and let some sun shine in? Or maybe just put a smile on your face? Make today a glossy day!

Goulash

Goulash is a mixture that can be boring or delicious. It's a stew that is made of beef or veal and vegetables AND paprika. It could be boring like leftovers, but if you add just the right amount of paprika, it's delicious. Life is like goulash. It's made up of ordinary stuff — like meat and vegetables and sometimes even leftovers. But if you add the spices of discovery, learning, friendship, music, prayer, and laughter, it can be delicious! Whenever you have a boring day, look around for some kind of spice to stir into your goulash of life — so you can make it a yummy day.

Grit

Grit can be fine particles of sand or stone — OR coarsely ground bits of grain like oats or wheat. When people are very determined to do something, they might grit their teeth together and stand firm, refusing to budge. You might say they have "true grit." Other people might grit their teeth — or grind them together — when they're angry or worried or nervous or scared. Did you know there's another word that's almost the same but means almost the OPPOSITE of grit? It's GRITH and it means peace, security, safety, refuge. So whenever you start to grit your teeth because you're upset about something, think about grith. Then say a little quiet prayer to ask God to help you find peace and safety. You can always find grith with God.

Grudge

Grudge is an ugly-sounding word that means to grumble, complain, envy (someone else's good luck), or show reluctance (to give something to someone). You might buy a birthday present for someone but want to KEEP it for yourself. When it comes time for the birthday party, you give the gift but instead of giving it happily or willingly, you give it grudgingly! OR you might be peeved at certain persons because they got something you didn't or did something you didn't like — so instead of forgiving and forgetting, you hang on to your anger and HOLD A GRUDGE against them. Grudges usually make you feel miserable, so they hurt YOU more than the person you are grudging. If YOU have been holding a grudge, get rid of it! Yuck! Throw it as far away as you can. Who would want to hold on to something so ugly!

Gum

Gum is something to chew. It exercises your jaws — and of course, everyone knows that exercise is GOOD for you! Some gums are flavored and taste good and even make your breath smell better. And some gums are even bubble-makers. So gum can be fun and maybe good for you too! But did you know that if it wasn't for a notorious military general, you might not have gum to chew? Many years ago Texas belonged to Mexico but WANTED to become part of the United States. There was a terrible battle in San Antonio, and the Mexican commander, Santa Anna, massacred everyone at the Alamo except two women and two children. In response, General Sam Houston led a force that defeated Santa Anna and forced Mexico to release Texas. After that, Santa Anna had to get out of Mexico, so he moved to Staten Island, New York, and he brought along his favorite "chew." It was called chicle and was the dried milky sap of the Mexican jungle tree known as the sapodilla. A New York inventor tried the General's chicle and decided he might invent a way to make money with it. He imported a big batch of chicle from Mexico and made it into little balls and put jars of them in drugstores where they were sold for a penny apiece. This new "chew" was a success, and later flavoring was added to make cherry, peppermint, and even sassafras gum. Today, there are many flavors and kinds of gum — and you owe it all to the notorious General who liked to chew while he slew! Now people like to chew while they watch a movie or ride a bike or take a walk. When do YOU like to chew gum and exercise your jaws? Does the exercise make you feel rested and relaxed and more peaceful than the General? Chew today on the thought of war and all the sadness it causes, then pray for world peace.

Gymnasiarch

In ancient Greece a gymnasiarch was a person appointed to supervise athletic games or contests. Maybe you have a gymnasiarch at YOUR school! Or maybe you have a gymnasium OR maybe you've gone to a gymnasium to exercise. What kind of exercise do you like best? Playing ball, swimming, jumping, running? How fast can you run? Did you know a cheetah can run seventy miles per hour for short distances? That's faster than the speed limit for cars on a highway! Of course, the cheetah has FOUR legs and YOU only have two! Why don't you use those two legs that God gave you and take a walk today? Walk down the street or around your back yard or in your house. Look at your watch and count how many steps you can take in five minutes. You may be surprised! If you KEEP exercising every day, maybe some day YOU can be a gymnasiarch!

 IS FOR...

Hello

Hello is a word you use when you're introduced to someone or when you see a friend at the mall or when you answer the phone. It can also be used when you are surprised or delighted. If you opened a letter and found a ten-dollar bill inside, you might say "HEL-LOOOO!" If you were a botanist and found a brand-new kind of flower under a shrub in the forest, you could say "HELL-OH!" If you were in the jungle and suddenly came upon a huge tiger, you could say "HELLOOO" — but you would probably say "HELLLP!" Different cultures and societies have used different words or gestures to greet one another through the ages. Some clubs have secret words or unusual handshakes that members use as a greeting. Soldiers salute officers. Japanese bow to one another. And they say Eskimos sometimes rub noses. And when Christians greet God in prayer, they often put their hands together and bow their heads. Of course, you don't have to use any SPECIAL way to speak to God — just like you don't have to use any special words or signals to say hello to a good friend.

Herb

Herb is a seed plant that is different from a tree or shrub because in the wintertime the herb's stem withers away, while the "stem" or trunk of the tree or shrub stays solid until the next spring when it sprouts new leaves. The flowers or seeds from herb plants — like sage, mint, or basil — are often used to flavor cooking. You've probably had turkey dressing flavored with sage, and spaghetti sauce flavored with several different herbs. But did you know that a banana is a herb? Yep. You probably thought that bananas grow on trees — but they don't! The banana is the largest known PLANT that grows without a woody stem or solid trunk. So the next time you have a banana split, you'll be eating ice cream with herbs! Imagine! An herb with a thick yellow skin that tastes delicious! Seems like the day God invented this plant, he really "went bananas."

Hobby

Hobby is a favorite way to pass the time, an enjoyable way to use spare time, something to do when there's nothing to do. The most popular hobby in the world is stamp collecting. Many people like to "collect" interesting or unusual TYPES of things — different types of shells, rocks, earrings, salt and pepper shakers, pens and pencils, hats. SOME people just collect dust balls under the bed! Other hobbies include games like golf, bowling, checkers, or chess. Did you know there are 170,000,000,000,000,000,000,000,000 ways to play the ten opening moves in a game of chess? That's what the experts say — so SOMEBODY must have spent a long time counting them all. Maybe counting was his or her hobby! Do YOU have a hobby? There are countless hobbies to choose from. So if you don't have one, why don't you spend today thinking of what hobby you would enjoy. How about crossword puzzles, reading, writing, knitting, or collecting hobby horses? There are probably 170,000,000,000,000,000,000,000,000 different hobbies you could choose. Isn't it exciting that life is so full of possibilities?

Hogwash

Hogwash is NOT something you do to your pig on Saturday night! This word is often used to explain empty talk, foolish ideas, or anything YOU don't agree with. When someone else expresses an opinion that is NOT the same as yours, you can say "HOGWASH" to let that person know you think he or she is just not as brilliant as you are. OR you could listen to the other person's opinion FIRST — before you say "hogwash." Who knows? You just might learn something! That's what often happens when you LISTEN and think and consider — instead of hogging the conversation!

Hot Dog

Hot dog could mean a puppy in the summertime OR that tasty meat-on-a-bun people enjoy at ball games. But do you know WHY a sandwich would be called a HOT DOG? Well there's a story — it may or may not be true — that many years ago there was a man who sold a new kind of sandwich at the ballpark, and he called it "tube steak with mustard"! Would you want to EAT something called tube steak? It sounds like it was made out of an old tire! But people tried it and LIKED it. The story goes that this tube-steak seller was always followed by his old collie dog. On those hot summer afternoons at the ballpark, the poor dog would start to wilt under his long collie hair, and he would pant and look VERY hot. Everybody noticed the hot dog and started calling his owner "the hot dog man"! Eventually, they started calling the hot dog man's sandwiches hot dogs! The next time you enjoy a yummy hot dog, be thankful for having lots of good things to eat, and the next time you see a hot collie, give that poor dog a drink of water!

Hut

Hut is a very small cabin or house, sometimes far away in the woods. Some people live in huts because they don't have enough money to live in a regular house. Some people live in huts only on weekends or vacations just to do something different, to "get away from it all" — whatever "it" is! The famous writer, George Bernard Shaw, had a special "writing hut" where he would go to be alone to write. HIS hut was built so it could spin on a pole to follow the sun! Wouldn't that be fun — to have a spinning hut! Well, wherever you live — in a house, a hut, a palace, or an apartment, enjoy it and appreciate it. Many homeless people would be happy to have ANY kind of shelter to get in from the cold and rain. So the next time you start to complain or feel bad because your home isn't big enough or fancy enough or warm enough or cool enough, stop and say a prayer of thanksgiving that you have SOME kind of hut to call HOME.

Hydroplane

Hydroplane is actually a BOAT — a small light motorboat with a special flat bottom that makes it possible for the boat to skim along the surface of the water at very high speeds. Doesn't that sound like fun — almost FLYING across water! Did you ever ride in a hydroplane? Did you like it? Or would you like it? Did you know *hydro* means water, and you can add it to other words to get new words and new meanings? HYDROPHONE is an instrument for listening to sound transmitted through water. HYDROSCOPE is an instrument you can use to look at things at great depths under the water. HYDROSTAT is an electrical device for measuring the level of water in a reservoir. Make a list today of all the words you can think of that have been made by taking two very different words and putting them together to make a new word! For starters, how about sun-screen? Foot-ball? Rail-road? Aren't words fun?

Hymn

Hymn is a festive song or a song praising or glorifying God. A hymn is usually sung in church, but it CAN be sung anywhere YOU are! Hymn is a funny-sounding name for a song, isn't it? It sounds like it can only be sung by hims and not hers! But it's called that because it came from the Latin word *hymnus* that MEANS song. We have a lot of English words that came from Latin words! If YOU had been naming a song to praise God, what would YOU have called it? Hooray? Wow? Loveya? Fantastic? Why don't you sing a hymn right now! If you don't KNOW any hymns, make up one! This is a good day for singing — because EVERY day is a good day for singing!

 IS FOR...

Idea

Idea is a thought, a notion, a plan, a scheme, an opinion, an intention. Wouldn't it be a good idea to come up with a good idea today? Think about it. Pray about it. Ask God to let a light bulb go off in your head and enLIGHTen your thoughts enough to help you think of a good idea — a way to solve a problem in your life, a plan to do something NEW with your life either today or waaay in the future, a goal, a project, a possibility. Dreams start with ideas, and "you gotta have a dream or you'll never have a dream come true."

Imagination

Imagination is having a LOT of ideas, a magic trick that lets you see something that isn't there, go somewhere you've never been, walk through a flower garden in the middle of a snowstorm, or go sledding on the hottest day of summer. Imagination is a special gift that humans have and animals don't. Imagination can save you from boredom, free you from ordinariness, change a drab day into a fun time, and maybe even change your whole life. Do YOU have a good imagination? Put it to work today. And enjoy.

Impeccable

Impeccable means without fault — so there are very few things OR people on earth who are impeccable. Actually, can you think of ANYthing that is perfect? Or ANYONE? It's good to TRY to be impeccable, but don't be too disappointed if you find a little smudge or a little fault in the people you know. They're only human. That's why they might do something you don't like ONCE in a while. If you expect impeccable, there's only one place to look — at your impeccable friend, God. Of course!

Impostor

Impostor is someone who pretends to be someone other than he or she really is. Some famous impostors have "posed" as doctors, although they never went to medical school; others have posed as stars, although they weren't! Do you know any persons who pretend to KNOW more than they really do or to be RICHER than they really are — or maybe even to be NICER than they really are? You might say these people wear masks even when it isn't Halloween! If you have any false-faced friends, either look for new friends or try to help your friends take off their masks. And if YOU have been POSING, then maybe it's time to take off YOUR mask too! Remember, God KNOWS who you really are and he wants you to act like yourself because you are his child — and God's child should NOT be wearing a false face!

Ink

Ink is that stuff inside your ballpoint pen that makes a mark when you jiggle the pen across a piece of paper. You're lucky to have such an easy way to write. Thousands of years ago if you wanted to write a message, you'd have to chisel letters into a block of stone or carve them into a tablet of wax or clay. And if you had to do that, you might not send many messages! Now there are ALL kinds of ink — permanent ink to use on documents, washable ink that will rinse out  of clothes, ink that is pink or blue or green or any color of the rainbow, and even ink that glows in the dark. Today, think about ink. Then USE some to write a note to somebody you love or would like to surprise. Make your mark! Get the message?

Invention

Invention is power — the power to imagine, envisualize, think of a way to do something in a way no one else has ever thought of before! There are many famous inventors and one of the MOST famous is Thomas Edison, the man who invented the phonograph so you could have recorded music and the electric light so you could have light without fire. But the phonograph and electric light are just TWO of the more than thirteen hundred inventions Edison patented. Many of his inventions were successful and made him famous BUT many MORE of his inventions DIDN'T work — so he knew about failure as well as success. Most lives have some failures and some successes — so rejoice in your successes and LEARN from your failures.

Isthmus

Isthmus is a small strip of land, bordered on both sides by water; it connects two large pieces of land. Did you know the Isthmus of Panama connects North America and South America? Even though it's small, an isthmus is very important because it CONNECTS. A safety pin is small but very important when you need one to hold something together. Sometimes YOU might feel small, but you are very important because you were made by God — and whatever God makes is important!

Ivy

Ivy is an evergreen plant that is a wanderer. Ivy roams all around the ground, but it's not TALL enough to see over a wall or even over a big rock. So what does it do? It climbs over them! It also climbs up the sides of houses and over fences. Though it's small and short, ivy really gets around! Since it isn't strong enough to support itself, it leans on something else! It gets its support from the rock or house or wall; and in return, it adds a bright touch of evergreen wherever it goes and grows. It does NOT take food from the one it leans on — like some parasite plants do. The ivy feeds itself but just LEANS on something taller, so it can grow up and out and all about. Everyone needs something to lean on sometimes. When you break a leg, you need a crutch. When you feel sad, you need a shoulder to cry on. It's good to be independent, but it's also nice to have someone to lean on, to depend on, once in a while. So when you wander and explore like the ivy, take along a friend to give you a hand to climb up a tree or over a fence. And when you come to a really rough spot, remember, you can ALWAYS lean on God.

 IS FOR...

Jack-in-the-box

Jack-in-the-box is a toy. JACK-IN-THE-PULPIT is a flower. JACK-O'-LANTERN is a pumpkin carved for Halloween. JACK RABBIT is a large rabbit with extra long ears. JACK SALMON is a fish. Do you know a PERSON named Jack? Jack is a popular nickname for the name John, and there have been many famous men in history named John or Jack. Why don't you get out a history book today and see HOW MANY famous Jacks you can find? Would YOU like to be a famous person in history some day? Well, maybe you will be!

Jellyfish

Jellyfish is a strange name for a sea animal but this IS a strange creature! It has a body made of a jellylike substance and is shaped like an umbrella or a pulsating parachute. When it washes up on shore, it looks like a slimy blob — but when it's photographed moving in the water, it looks like a creature of fragile beauty. Swimmers who are unlucky enough to step on a jellyfish that has washed up on the shore never forget — because they get a painful poisonous sting. Underwater divers who see jellyfish never forget either because they get a glimpse of strange, alien-looking creatures that come in many varieties, brilliant colors, and spectacular shapes. Think today about the amazing VARIETY of the creatures God made to fill his universe — the huge hippopotamus and the tiny hummingbird, the long-necked giraffe and the almost no-neck bulldog, the kangaroo with a pocket on its tummy, and the pelican with a pocket in its bill! Thank God for letting you live in such a varied, never-boring world.

Jetsam

Jetsam sounds like it might have something to do with jet travel but it doesn't. In fact this is one word that hardly ever travels alone! You usually hear it joined with another word — in the phrase "flotsam and jetsam." Back in the days when people AND cargo journeyed across the ocean in big ships — instead of in jets — the word *flotsam* meant the cargo or the parts of a wrecked ship that FLOATED on the water. But *jetsam* described things that had been THROWN OVERBOARD — to make the ship lighter so that it would not sink OR with the hope that the cargo would float instead of going down with the ship. This might not seem like an important difference to YOU, but it was back then! According to their laws, flotsam that could be scooped out of the water by another ship would then belong to the country where the ship came from. But jetsam that could be brought to shore belonged to the OWNER of the ship. Today, we often use the term "flotsam and jetsam" to refer to the unfortunate homeless people who seem to be drifting because their lives have been "wrecked" by some storm or because they have been "thrown away" by society. Say a prayer today for all homeless people and think if there is any way you or your family or your community could do anything to help them find their way safely back to shore.

Jigsaw

Jigsaw is a special saw that can cut wood in curvy or irregular lines, and a JIGSAW PUZZLE is a picture that has been cut into curvy or irregular lines so you can have the fun of putting it back together again. Do you know who made the first jigsaw puzzle? Well, more than two hundred years ago there was a man named John Spilsbury who thought it would be fun to teach geography by playing a game. He took slabs of wood and painted maps on them; then he cut the maps along the boundary lines of the countries or states. Instead of just HEARING about geography, his class had the fun of trying to figure out where each country fit into the puzzle. Since then, there have been all kinds of jigsaw puzzles — some with just a few pieces for small children and some with five thousand pieces for people who really like to get it all together. Do YOU like jigsaw puzzles? You can make your own, you know. Just draw a picture, then cut it into irregular pieces and see if you can put it back together. Do you guess that's how God made the world — putting a mountain here, a river there? No, guess not. But it sounds like fun, doesn't it?

Jitterbug

Jitterbug is the silly name for a silly-looking dance. When you jitterbug, you jump around like a nervous or jittery bug! You might LOOK silly, but it's still fun to dance and jump around with music. People have been doing that since the first native learned how to bang two sticks together or blow through a wooden tube or reed to

make music. And there are WORSE bugs than jitterbugs. Litterbugs leave messy stuff all over the house and the planet. Bugs that are viruses make people sick. And crawly bugs bite you and make you itch and tickle you with their crawly feet. Of course, there are NICE bugs too. One is called a praying mantis — and a praying bug MUST be a nice bug. Another is called a ladybug, so it MUST have nice manners. And then there's the Volkswagen "bug," a nickname for a cute little car. How many OTHER bugs can you name?

Junction

Junction is a joining, a combining, OR a crossing place where two things come together — like where two highways or two railroads cross each other. There are a lot of "junctions" in life where things either come together or cross and go off into different directions. And some people have more junctions than others. Some people live in the same house for years, and others come to junctions and move to a new house, a new city, or maybe even a new country. Some friends stay friends for years and years, and others stay friends for a short while and then come to a junction and go off in different directions. Staying can be safe and secure OR boring. New directions can be scary OR exciting. It all depends on how you feel about it. Security is good and so is excitement, and MOST lives have a little of both. Look for some junctions in your neighborhood today. How many streets cross, how many paths? How many "cross" people do you cross? Think about junctions and which path YOU would like to take to the future.

K IS FOR...

Ketchup

Ketchup is a word that is sometimes spelled CATSUP. You KNOW what it is — it's that red stuff you pour on French fries or hamburgers. People disagree about how to spell it, but most people AGREE that it makes certain foods taste better when you pour it on! Ketchup is made of tomatoes and spices and is one of the reasons that YOU may eat twenty-two pounds of tomatoes each year! That's right! Statistics show that most Americans eat about twenty-two pounds of tomatoes every year — but that includes tomatoes you eat in salads PLUS the ones used in ketchup and spaghetti sauce and other good tomatoey things. These bright red beautiful "ketchup vegetables" are just one of the many delicious things God planted in the garden of Earth. If you haven't been eating enough tomatoes, maybe it's time for you to KETCH UP!

Kite

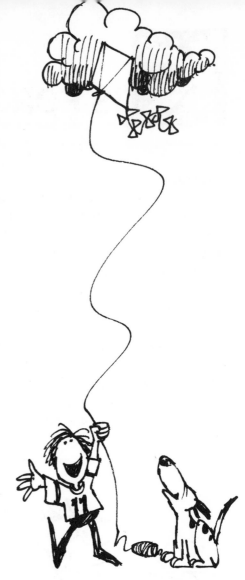

Kite is a toy, a thing of beauty, a way to fly without wings. It's also a word used in a funny American expression. When someone wants you to "get lost," they might say, "Awww, go fly a kite!" Actually, they'd be telling you to do something nice because kiteflying is fun! BUT did you know that same expression used in Spain would be, "Go fly an asparagus!" Isn't that a funny idea? An asparagus is a funny-looking vegetable that would be hard to describe — just like a kite is hard to describe! You almost have to SEE one to understand what it is. A kite can be lots of different shapes and sizes and colors, but it CAN be just two lightweight sticks of wood (one long, one short) tied together like a cross and then covered with paper or cloth. ALL kites have a looooong string so you can take the kite outside on a windy day, run with it, and hold onto the string while the kite soars high, high into the air while you stand on the ground, holding the string and watching it FLY like a beautiful bird. Sometimes you might WISH that you could fly with the wind like the kite OR you might just be happy to stay in your own backyard and enjoy watching the flight. Say a prayer today to thank God for the wonderful gift of wind — for the breeze that can cool your face on a hot summer day or make your kite fly high into the sky. But — even on the windiest day — never ever try to fly an asparagus!

Kittle

Kittle is NOT a cooking pot. This is a word that means "to tickle or puzzle." Do YOU ever like to tickle or puzzle someone? If you do, ask somebody if he or she knows what a "kleenebok" is. No, it is not what happens when you take a bath and scrub your back clean. A kleenebok is an animal — a small antelope of South Africa. See how easy it is to "puzzle" someone? Look up some other strange words in your dictionary (either this *Fun Facts Dictionary* or a regular dictionary) and then see how many people you can trick by asking them the meaning of a word they don't know, but YOU do!

Knickknack

Knickknack is a thing that is more ornamental than useful, a thing that looks nice sitting around the house but doesn't DO anything. Does that describe anybody in your family? Well, it wouldn't be nice to suggest that because a knickknack is really a THING, not a

person! It's a little doo-dad, a whatchamacallit, a bauble, a "valuable" piece of junk! But it can be fun to collect knickknacks even if they aren't useful. The world is full of things that WORK a lot — refrigerators, lamps, cars, dishwashers, televisions. They're workers. But it's fun to have unworkers too. Do YOU have any knickknacks in your room — or in your pocket? Why do you like them even if they don't DO anything? Maybe it's the same reason God loves you even when YOU don't DO anything — because you're special to him.

Knot

Knot is something you tie in a thread or a rope or the ribbon on a Christmas present. There are lots of WAYS to tie a knot and some knots even have special names according to the way they are tied. Did you know that? Here are some knotty names: thief knot, granny knot, clove hitch, cat's-paw, sheepshank, rolling hitch, outside clinch, and Englishman's tie. Do you know how to tie any of those knots? Do you know any OTHER kind of knots? Well, when two people get married, it's called "tying the knot"; when people are very nervous or worried, they might get a "knot in the stomach"; a hole in a board is called a "knothole" because it's the place where a knot of wood has fallen out; and when you get in a lot of trouble, you have a "knotty" problem. If you ever get "all tied up" so you're too busy to do chores at home or say your prayers or help a neighbor or just sit down and have a good giggle, you better hurry and get yourself UNtied. Being all tied up is KNOT a good way to spend a life!

Knuckle

Knuckle is the place where your finger bends when you make a fist. KNUCKLE BALL is something a baseball pitcher throws; KNUCKLEHEAD might be someone who doesn't know how to throw a knuckle ball; KNUCKLE SANDWICH is what you get when a guy hits you in the mouth with his fist because you called him a knucklehead! So be careful whom you call a knucklehead and be careful to know when NOT to knuckle under. When you KNOW you're right about something important (like not using drugs or cheating or stealing), you shouldn't knuckle under just because some knucklehead WANTS you to do something stupid.

L IS FOR LAW

Law

Law is a rule, a principle, a formula, a commandment. Laws are necessary — especially in school, at home, on the highway, AND in your heart. But some of the OLD laws sound funny to us now. Did you know at one time it was against the law to take a bath more than once a month! And it was illegal to build a fire under a mule or to ride on a streetcar after you ate garlic! Those laws sound funny now, but all of them were probably passed for good reasons. Most families have laws that were made for good reasons too. Sometimes the laws change because situations change, but sometimes they DON'T change even though children in the family WANT them to change. Do you know which set of laws has NOT changed for hundreds and hundreds of years? That's right! God's Ten Commandments. Do you KNOW what the Ten Commandments are? If you were making laws, would you make more than ten? What laws would YOU make?

Library

Library is a room or a building where books are kept for reading or for reference. Do YOU ever go to a library and browse for a book to take home? Well, what if the library had to come to YOU? And what if it came by bus or airplane? In some places where there are no libraries nearby, people go to "bookmobiles." These are often buses that have been equipped with shelves full of books. The bus is driven to some neighborhood and parked. Then people come to get new books or return books they had gotten on the last visit — just like you do at a regular library. But in Alaska, books come by plane! Some people live so far away from any town that they have to SKI to a drop-off point where green mailbags full of books are dropped off for them from an airplane! Those people LOVE to read and can't WAIT to get new books each time the book plane comes. Do YOU like to read? Reading is a window on the world, a gateway to adventure, a path to knowledge — and it's fun too! You're off to a good start because you're reading THIS book, but don't stop here! Read for discovery AND enjoyment. You'll never be too old to learn something new!

Lightning

Lightning is an exciting zigzag flash in the sky that you see before or during a thunderstorm. This exciting light jumps from one part of a cloud to another or leaps from cloud to cloud. And while it is racing across the sky, lightning heats the air along its path to temperatures as high as fifty-four thousand degrees Fahrenheit. Wow! Can you imagine anything that HOT? Then the air explodes into waves and you HEAR those waves! What do they sound like? Like a slow rumble or a sharp clap. Yep, wavy thunder! Do you like to watch a storm? It can be fun — as long as you watch from a window INSIDE a nice dry comfy room.

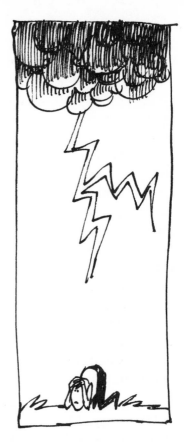

Link

Link is a ring or a loop that is part of a chain. Each link is important, and ALL the links need to be strong and held tight together to make a good chain. That's the same way it is with a team or a club or a family or a church. Each "link" must work with the others and help the others and hold tight together — whether there are only two links in the chain or two hundred. Are YOU a good link — or a missing link?

Llama

Llama is a graceful, regal-looking animal that moves like a dancer and spits like a baseball player! Llamas are lovable — most of the time. Some people think they are perfect pets. But they DO have that one bad habit of spitting. Fortunately, they usually only spit at other llamas, but they like to look DOWN on people. A llama will climb on a rock to be taller than its owner. If the owner also climbs on a rock and holds a hand in the air, the llama will see the hand is higher and give up and walk away as if to say, "Okay, you're the boss." But the next day the llama will climb up on the rock again! Do you know anybody who is always climbing, trying to act bigger or better than somebody else? Do you ever do that? It's good to always try to do your best, but it's NOT good to always try to TOP others. Today, instead of climbing, adopt a different llama habit. Walk gracefully like a dancer. Act regal. Be lovable. But don't spit!

Loser

Loser is someone who loses things OR it can be the opposite of winner. For example, a winner is someone who says, "This is not easy, but I bet if I work on it really hard, I can do it." A loser says, "I give up." A winner respects someone who is "in charge" (like a parent, a teacher, or a group leader) and tries to LEARN from that person. A loser resents authority, always criticizes any leader, and NEVER learns. A winner says, "They only have hot dogs on this picnic and I don't like hot dogs but I DO like picnics and outdoor games and being with friends, so I'm gonna have a good time anyway." A loser says, "I hate hot dogs, so I'm going home." Do you know any losers? Do you know any winners? Which one do you think will have a happier life? Which one will YOU be?

Luggage

Luggage is another name for baggage, or suitcases, that you LUG around on a trip. Some people carry around luggage even when they're not on a trip. They remember something mean somebody did to them a looooong time ago. They think about the time they wanted to go somewhere and didn't get to go. They fret about a special present they ALWAYS wanted and NEVER got. They concentrate on all the BAD things that ever happened to them and forget all the good. And they lug these unhappy thoughts around with them wherever they go. NEVER be a lugger. Forgive the bad things and FORGET them. Then you'll be FREE to enjoy traveling around as free as a bird — with NO bad thoughts, no mean memories, no unhappy feelings. You'll be free to be happy!

Lyre

Lyre is a musical instrument that does NOT tell lies but DOES make beautiful music. It looks and sounds a bit like a harp, and it was used by the ancient Greeks to make background music for singers and reciters. Reciters would SPEAK rather than SING. They would recite poetry, read a few pages from a book, or act out a part of a play while the lyre played in the background. If you're ever tempted to tell a lie, think of the lyre and make beautiful music by reciting the truth instead of making a liar of yourself!

 IS FOR...

Magnet

Magnet is a piece of steel or metal that has the ability to "attract" other pieces of steel or metal. Do you have any magnets on your refrigerator? A lot of people use little magnets to hold notes, recipes, and photographs on the refrigerator so they can see them as they pass through the kitchen each day. But have you noticed that some PEOPLE are also magnets? They seem to "attract" other people, to draw people to themselves. Do you know why? Usually the "magnetic" people are very friendly or generous or helpful or fun to be around. Do you know any magnetic people? Wasn't it nice of God to make people like that so others can enjoy being with them? Think today of all the magnetic people you know — and what you could do to be a magnet too!

Mail

Mail includes letters, boxes, and packages that are delivered from one place to another by the post office. Years ago there was only the pony express, and men rode ponies from city to city, post office to post office, to deliver the mail. Today, there is an elaborate postal service that uses buses, trains, trucks, and airplanes to take mail across town or across the world. But you have to PAY to get your mail delivered today. Before 1863 the postal service in the United States was FREE! Do you know of ANYTHING that is free today? Think about that. The air you breathe, the sunshine that warms you, the breeze that cools you, the wildflowers in the forest, and joy and laughter are ALL FREE. God made them and gave them to you. So help yourself to something FREE today!

Medicine

Medicine is a concoction to help you feel better — to treat a troubled tummy, to cure a cough, to dry up a drippy nose, to force out a fever, to soothe a sore toe. Did you know SOME people think the BEST medicine is chocolate? Oh, yes, they do. No matter how bad they feel, chocolate can make them feel much better. Once there was an Aztec ruler named Montezuma, and the people in his "court" (the officials or people who lived in his palace) drank TWO THOUSAND pitchers of chocolate EVERY DAY! Now that's a lot of chocolate! What do YOU do when you feel bad? What makes you feel better? Say a prayer today for all the people who are sick or lonely or just feel bad or sad. If you KNOW someone like that, why don't you try to help by giving that person a chocolate bar or a chocolate cookie or a nice smile?

Metal

Metal is a natural material like iron, aluminum, or gold. Many things are made of metal such as iron gates, aluminum pots, and gold rings. Did you know that PURE gold is so soft that you could mold it with your hands the way you mold things out of clay? Those who work with gold have to add a bit of copper to it so it will be strong enough to hold its shape when used to make jewelry and rings. Pure silver is very soft too, so copper is added to it before it's used to make knives and forks and fancy silver bowls. There's a saying that "new friends are silver, old friends are gold." Which do you like better — silver or gold, new friends or old friends? They're BOTH great, aren't they? Spend some time today with a new friend or an old friend and talk about metals. Pick out one metal and see how many things you can name that could be made from it.

Microscope

Microscope is an instrument made of lenses that magnify so you can get a better look, a magnified look, at any tiny object — like a leaf, a bug, a drop of water. Something too small to be examined by the human eye can be seen clearly by looking at it through the lens of the microscope. Did you know people began using glass lenses to see better waaay back in 1300? Almost three hundred years later a Dutch family, the Janssens, tried putting one lens over another in a tube and invented the compound microscope. Then, in 1660 another Dutchman named Anton Van Leeuwenhoek started using microscopes to study bacteria and found how useful this "tool" could be in scientific study. Since then, microscopes have been improved and are used in classes by students as well as by scientists. And many amazing discoveries have been made in the fields of science and biology — thanks to the microscope. Have YOU ever used a microscope? It's amazing how different things look when they're magnified and seen "up close." Even the wing of a fly or the petal of a flower has an intricate special design that you would never see at a glance. Some people are like that too. You have to look at them very closely and get to know them "up close" before you realize how special they are. Look at someone closely today and see if you've been missing something special about that person.

Mineral

Mineral is something that is NOT animal or vegetable. Did you know that all "natural" things can be put in three general classifications: animal, vegetable, or mineral? Since YOU are not a vegetable or a mineral but you ARE natural, that makes you an animal! But a very nice special animal! Minerals are often found waaaaay underground, and people have to build mines to dig down and get to them. Minerals sometimes mix in with underground water, and some people think this mineral water is very good for you, so they go to places where there are sulphur springs and drink the water or take baths in it. BUT sulphur water has an awful smell and taste. One man who took a "curative" bath in sulphur water said it CURED him of ever wanting to take another one! Did you ever smell sulphur water? If you did, you would never forget it — and you probably wouldn't want to smell it again. How many minerals can you name? How many vegetables? How many animals? There are so many surprising things in and on the earth. Which ones do you think are most important — animals, vegetables, or minerals?

Mirror

Mirror is that thing you look into and say, "Mirror, mirror, on the wall, who is the cutest one of all?" The FIRST mirror was a clear pool of water or maybe a lake or a river! A lady looked in the water and saw a FACE — a face she had never seen before! That must have been a scary surprise! But thirty-five hundred years BEFORE Jesus was born, people learned how to make mirrors from polished metal. The Romans had mirrors of polished silver and gold. But it was not until 1300 that the first glass mirrors — or looking glasses — were made. Do you look in the mirror a lot? What do you see? A frown or a smile? Did you know the WORLD is like a mirror? If you frown at the world, it will frown right back. And then you'll feel angry and sad. Smile at the world and SEE the good side of it — and the world will smile back at you!

Molecule

Molecule is a minute particle, a teeny-tiny bit of something. For instance, the air you breathe is made up of molecules that are always changing as the wind blows, the earth turns, the sun goes down, and the moon comes up! Since nature continually recycles the air, they SAY that YOU may be breathing some of the same molecules of air once breathed by Michelangelo or Babe Ruth or Abraham Lincoln or maybe even Jesus! Isn't that an interesting idea? Other than Jesus, who do you think was the most exciting person who ever lived? Who would you like to have a conversation with? Whose air would you like to breathe?

Mosquito

Mosquito is a buzzy bug that bites. Ouch! If you live in an air-conditioned house, you have your windows closed so you probably only have to worry about mosquitoes when you go on picnics or camping trips. But people in many parts of the world — especially those who live near a river — get buzzed so much that they have to use something called "mosquito netting" so they can sleep at night. Mosquitoes can't fly through or bite through this net, so people either wrap up in it or drape it over their beds at night. Have you ever slept under mosquito netting? Have you ever been bitten by a mosquito? They're pesky little critters, aren't they? Do you know any people who act like mosquitoes, buzzing around and biting at people by making fun of others or making "biting," mean remarks about them? YOU would never act like a mosquito, would you?

 **IS FOR...**

Name

Name is the title or word or phrase by which a person or a thing is known. A person's LAST name is the family name — like Smith or Jones or Abercrombie. The FIRST name is the special one chosen when the person was born — to identify him or her — like John or Mary or Aloysius or Lucretia. Do you LIKE your name? Do you WISH you could have a different one? SOME names seem to be just perfect for a person — like a girl named Daisy who is always bright and perky and happy-looking like a daisy! Other names don't seem quite right. Did you ever think that since you are a Christian, you are a "namesake" of Christ? Does that name suit you? Do you act like Christ did — all the time, sometimes, once in a while? Even "once in a while" means you're trying! Think about names today — the ones you like or DON'T like, the ones that sound pretty OR funny, the ONE name that might suit you best!

Napkin

Napkin is a small piece of paper or cloth that you use to wipe your messy mouth or sticky fingers when you're having a meal or a snack. But did you know napkins were once the size of TOWELS? Well, forks and knives hadn't been invented yet, so people ate huge meals using only their fingers — and they NEEDED towels to wipe their hands. They also used "finger bowls" — bowls filled with flower-scented water — so they could wash their hands before they left the table. At one time napkins were also used like "doggy bags"! When a banquet ended, guests would wipe their hands and then wrap up leftovers in the napkin to take home. And it was considered BAD manners to leave without your napkin! The word *napkin* came from a French word that meant "little tablecloth." The British used this word to describe a large cloth which they tied around the waist like an apron — so they could protect their clothes while they ate and have something on which to wipe their hands. Through the years a napkin has been a towel, a tablecloth, and an apron! When YOU enjoy a nice meal, PLEASE don't wipe your hands on the kitchen towel, tablecloth, or apron. That could cause distress, disgust, and discussion. Be polite and mannerly — USE A NAPKIN!

Nasturtium

Nasturtium is a funny name for an interesting flower. The name comes from two Latin words which literally mean "nose-twist." That's because this flower has a powerful aroma — SO powerful that if you breathe in the pungent scent, you might feel like somebody has twisted your nose! Some people like to EAT nasturtiums in a salad. Would YOU ever eat a flower? If you do, be VERY careful — some flowers are poisonous! Would you ever twist someone's nose? If you do, be VERY careful — some people who get noses twisted, twist back in a very poisonous way! The next time you're in a flower store look for a nasturtium or a package of nasturtium seeds. You may be surprised at how pretty this nose-twisting flower is. Isn't it exciting that nature has so many surprises, so many twists and turns? There's always something new to discover — around the world or around the corner!

Neon

Neon is the gas used to make the bright neon signs you often see on restaurants, theaters, or stores. Strangely enough, neon itself is colorless! But some chemists discovered that when you put neon in a tube and pass electricity through it, it glows with a bright red-orange color! Later, they added mercury vapors to the neon and got MORE colors. Today, tubes are shaped to form letters and designs, and neon signs glow with all sorts of shapes and colors. Some people seem "colorless" and boring like colorless neon, but they CHANGE when something is added — something like kindness, friendship, or a helping hand. Do you know anyone who is colorless? Would you like to try to help that person change?

Nictitate

Nictitate has nothing to do with nicking a potato or a secret-coded message from "Nick to Tate." Nope. This is a fancy word that means WINK! Yes, it does. No joke. When you nictitate, you wink or blink. Did YOU ever nictitate? Some birds wink and blink faster than you can count. Some people wink when they make a joke or when they're trying to get

your attention. Look out the window today and wink one eye as fast as you can. Then blink BOTH eyes as fast as you can. You'll see the world jumping up and down, really MOVING! Did you know that's the way the very FIRST "movies" looked? In old movies everything MOVED in a very funny, jiggly way. Now close both eyes TIGHTLY, and then open them real fast and pretend you are an ALIEN who has just landed on Earth. You have never ever seen anything like this before on YOUR planet. You've never seen such colors or shapes or plants or people. Everything you touch or taste or smell or hear is brand new. Spend all day being an alien and exploring this fascinating planet known as EARTH. And if anyone asks what you're doing, just nictitate and say, "I'm discovering a new world."

Nightshade

Nightshade is not a shade you pull down at night. It's a family of flowering plants! And it's a very strange family. The nightshade is related to the potato and tomato, yet one type of this plant is known as the DEADLY nightshade because it's poison. Another variety is known as the stinking nightshade. Don't ask why! Isn't it strange how some plants can be related to one another and yet are SO different? Have you noticed that some family members are like that too? Even those in the same family can look, talk, and behave very differently. That's because each person is unique — maybe similar to others but never the same. God must have a great imagination to make each and every person who has ever been or ever will be on the earth UNIQUE!

No

No is the word that means the opposite of YES. It can be good to say no. Or it can be a mistake. Are you very careful about the decisions you make? Do you sometimes say no when you should say yes or say yes when you should say no? Think about that today.

Norm

This is a word that could be a boy's name OR it could mean a rule, a pattern, or an idea of the way people in a certain group are expected to look or act or think. If you follow the "norm," you are "normal" or average or just like all the other people. BUT if you look or act or think in a different way, this does NOT mean that you are NOT normal. It just means that you are YOU. For example, did you know that a giraffe has seven bones in its neck — exactly the same number of bones that a mouse has in its neck? But the giraffe's neck does NOT look or act like the mouse's neck. Both are normal but both are different. So be grateful for the way God made you — a lot like other people but also a lot different! And always try to be the BEST you that you can be!

 **IS FOR...**

Obbligato

Obbligato is a word used in music to indicate something that is indispensable, something that CAN'T be left out. Do YOU ever feel left out? You shouldn't — because to God, YOU are indispensable. There never has been and never will be another you! So the next time you feel left out, useless, or unimportant, just tell yourself, "To God, I am an obbligato!"

Odoriferous

Odoriferous is a fancy name that describes something that smells! But it smells GOOD — like an odoriferous flower or spice. God made so many odoriferous things — which are your favorites? A rose, a gardenia, honeysuckle, cinnamon, nutmeg, popcorn? Did you say an onion? No, an onion is NOT odoriferous, although it DOES have an odor!

Onion

Onion is a strange vegetable that can make you smile or make you cry! Some people who LOVE onions might SMILE when they're served a meatloaf or stew or casserole made with lots of onion flavor. Some people might CRY when they have to PEEL the onions to put into those recipes. Do you know why peeling an onion can make you cry? Well, when you cut an onion, it releases a special chemical in the air. This chemical reacts with the moisture on the surface of your eyes and forms a weak solution of sulfuric ACID! When the acid starts to sting, your eyes fight back! They produce tears to dilute the acid and wash it away! Isn't it amazing how your body always reacts to danger and fights back to protect you? The next time you peel an onion, give yourself some EXTRA protection — wear swim goggles! (Won't you look funny wearing swim goggles in the kitchen?) And then say a prayer to thank God for making such swimmingly sensational things as onions and eyes!

Orange

Orange is a citrus fruit you squeeze to get juice for breakfast. Right? Well, not exactly. Botanically speaking, an orange is a berry! Did you know you've been drinking berry juice for breakfast? Well, so what — as long as it tastes berry good! Have you ever looked at the way an orange is made? It's all in sections, so you can just pull it apart and don't even need a knife to separate it. Wasn't it nice of God to SLICE it for you?

Orangutan

Orangutan sounds like it might be related to the orange, but it certainly isn't! An orangutan is an ape that is almost as large as a gorilla. The only thing about an orangutan that might be like an orange is its hair, which is a reddish-brown and might LOOK orange! Did you ever see an orangutan at the zoo? Isn't it fun to go to the zoo and see all the animals — and let all the animals see YOU? Do you guess they think YOU are as funny as you think they are?

Ore

Ore is something that has a surprise in it! It's in the ground or under the ground and you can get stuff like iron, gold, or diamonds from it! IF you know how! And IF you are willing to work really hard at it. Did you know you would have to unearth two hundred fifty TONS of ore to get a one-carat diamond? (Diamonds are measured in "carats" instead of pounds or tons! A one-carat diamond would be about twice as big as the ones you usually see in a girl's engagement ring.) That explains why you can't go out and dig up a diamond any time you want one. MOST things that are valuable take a lot of "digging" to get — like a college diploma, a medical degree, a million dollars, a happy family, a good friend. How good are you at digging?

Owl

Owl is the name of a bird that asks "Who? Who?" instead of "Why? Why?" — the question most children ask! There are several different kinds of owls, including the great horned owl, the screech owl, and the barn owl. The barn owl DOESN'T "hoot" like other owls. Instead, it makes a hoarse *khurrew* noise. It has telescopic vision and can hunt at night in total darkness because of its superb sense of hearing. In fact, the barn owl's ears are so sensitive that they are surrounded by small feathered flaps that can be closed over the delicate inner parts of the ear when there's too much noise. Wouldn't YOU like to have flaps to shut out the noise of someone fussing at you or asking you to do something you don't WANT to do? Or maybe it would be better if your FAMILY had flaps over

their ears so they could shut out the noise YOU make! Listen today for all the tiny little noises that an owl might hear but YOU might miss. Listen to what people say too — just in case they've been TRYING to tell you something important but you weren't listening. Then thank God for the wonderful gift of ears.

 IS FOR...

Paper Clip

Paper clip is a twisted piece of wire that can be used to hold several pieces of paper together so they won't get lost or blow away in the wind or fall into your soup. This clip was invented more than ninety years ago (in 1900). Wonder what people used to keep their papers together before then? Maybe they rolled 'em up and tied 'em with a string! Do you ever have a day when you feel rolled up or all "strung out"? When you just can't seem to "get it all together"? Maybe somebody said something about you that wasn't nice and you feel bad. Or you want to go someplace and can't and you're disappointed. Or you have so many chores to do, you'll never have time to finish and it's not fair! Well, just PRETEND you are writing each worry on one piece of paper. Then paper-clip all your worries together and pitch 'em out the window or toss 'em in the trash or send 'em into orbit! And THEN — since you won't have to spend all day worrying about your problems — you'll have all that extra time to get those chores finished!

Peanut Butter

Peanut butter is a gooey brown paste made by grinding peanuts together. It looks yucky and tastes yummy. It sticks to bread and sometimes it sticks to the roof of your mouth too! If you like peanut-butter sandwiches, you can thank George Washington Carver, a man who discovered lots of ways to use peanuts, sweet potatoes, and soybeans. Carver was born into a black slave family around the time of the Civil War. When he grew up, he became an agricultural chemist and did RESEARCH, which led to the discovery of ways to improve crops and make synthetic products out of things like potatoes and wood. His many innovations helped improve the economy of the South, and he became a real hero of science! You wouldn't think studying a peanut could make you a hero, would you? But it did! Look around today and find some little ORDINARY thing to study or think about — a pencil, a sock, a book, a little brother. Make a list of all the GOOD things this little ordinary thing brings to everyday life — yes, even a little brother. And thank God for ALL things, great and small.

Perihelion

Perihelion is that point in the orbit of a planet or comet when it is NEAREST the Sun. The APHELION is when it is FARTHEST from the Sun. Since the Earth travels in an oval rather than a circle around the Sun, it is sometimes farther and sometimes closer. BUT when it is the closest, at its perihelion, it is STILL 91,400,000 miles away! Did you ever sunbathe by a pool and feel like you must be VERY near the sun? No matter how hot you got, you were AT LEAST 91,400,000 miles away! Isn't God's universe amazing — with planets, comets, stars, galaxies, AND people? Aren't ALL God's creations amazing! Always remember — YOU are one of those creations and YOU are amazing!

Physician

Physician is another name for a doctor, a healer, someone who studies about medicine and uses it to help sick people. A legendary Greek healer, Asclepius, was pictured with a snake and a staff (or a tall stick) hundreds of years ago, and that symbol is still used today for the medical profession. Think today about "symbols" — things that are used to identify something. You see lots of them on TV to identify products, but there are other kinds of symbols too. The picture of an apple is often used to illustrate the teaching profession. When you see a pumpkin, you think of Halloween; a heart reminds you of Valentine Day. What do you think of when you see a cross? Most people think of Jesus. What symbol would best identify YOU? A schoolbook, a baseball bat, a piano, a hamburger, a rainbow? Think about it.

OINK

Pig

Pig is a young swine, an oinker, a surprisingly smart animal that has been VERY useful to people for a very long time. Archaeologists say there were tame pigs in China over six thousand years ago! Historians say that Hernando De Soto brought the first pigs to America when he landed in Florida in 1539. Scientists say pigs have been very useful in the field of medicine because they have been used in experiments on diabetes, alcoholism, and heart disease. Manufacturers say pigskin is great for making shoes, gloves, and billfolds. And people who like to eat bacon or sausage or pork chops say pigs are delicious! Yep, it seems the lowly pig has been a BIG help to society — in lots of ways. Have you ever tried to insult someone by calling him or her a PIG? Has anyone ever called YOU a pig? Think about it. Considering all the good things pigs do for people, maybe it would be a bigger insult to call a pig a person! Maybe you should say a prayer today to thank God for that great and wonderful animal — the pig!

Potato

Potato is a valuable vegetable — because without it you couldn't have potato chips! Do you know who first cooked potato chips? It was a chef named George Crum — and he had a crummy reason for coming up with the chip idea! He was angry! Crum had served French fries to a customer who complained the fries were "too thick and soggy and not salty enough." Crum thought the fries were just right and the customer was all wrong, so he decided to SHOW that crabby customer. He grabbed a sharp knife and sliced a potato in paper-thin slices so it would not be "too thick," and then he soaked the slices in ice water so they would be crunchy. Next, he fried the slices until they were brown and crispy, and then he poured on LOTS of salt. He was sure the customer would HATE these potato "chips." But you know what happened, don't you? The customer LOVED them! And he kept talking about them, and soon people were coming into the restaurant ASKING for Crum's "chips." The news spread and today the average American eats about FOUR POUNDS of potato chips a year. That means they're really "in the chips"! And they owe it all to a crabby customer and a grumpy chef. Is there some vegetable you DON'T like? Maybe you could think of a way to cook it in a different way and discover something delicious. How about chocolate-covered zucchini, squash ice cream, spinach cake? No, better think some more. Maybe YOU can come up with an idea just as good as Mr. Crum's.

President

President is the title for someone who is the head honcho, the top gun, the leader, the one in the "hot seat," the top official of a company or a country. You know that George Washington was the FIRST president of the United States of America, but did you know that he had trouble with his wind-blown hair? Back in George's time most men wore wigs! Yes, they did! And they were WHITE wigs! Well, George was proud of his thick healthy hair and refused to wear a wig. Instead, he would comb white powder into his hair so it would LOOK like he was wearing a white wig. The only problem was that George had to travel places on horseback; he couldn't call a cab, hop on a bus, or take a jet! As he rode, the wind would blow the powder out of his hair. Poor George was always having to stop and

"powder his head." See? Even presidents have problems! Would YOU like to be a president some day? Would you like to ride horseback? Or wear a wig? Think today of all the things you might like to DO or BE some day. And then get started! It takes work — and prayer — to turn thoughts into reality.

Pretzel

Pretzel is a twisty, salty snack that was first made to look like arms folded in prayer and was given to children as a reward for learning certain prayers. Those pretzels were soft because they were only baked a short time like rolls. But THEN one day a young "apprentice" baker was left to watch the oven, and you know what happened? HE FELL ASLEEP. When he woke up, the pretzels had been baked to a crisp. His boss came in and saw what had happened and was furious. He shouted and scolded and grabbed up one of the pretzels and bit into it to prove how awful it was — BUT — it wasn't awful! It was crunchy and delicious. Ever since, there have been soft pretzels AND crunchy ones — thanks to a sleepy baker boy. The next time you eat a pretzel, fold your arms and say a prayer for bakers AND for sleepy, tired workers everywhere.

Purple Martin

Purple martin is the name of a bird that isn't really purple but IS a dragon killer! The male bird might look a LITTLE purple but it's really a blue-black color and the female bird is grayish. They've become very popular birds because they LIKE to eat mosquitoes. Since people LIKE to get rid of mosquitoes, the martins might be called "purple people pleasers"! These little birds also eat flies and wasps, but their very most FAVORITE food is — guess what? DRAGONFLIES! Imagine! Birds that slay dragons! (And you thought only knights on white horses did that!) Have you ever SEEN a dragon? Have you ever seen a dragonfly? Have you ever seen a purple martin? Have you ever thought about how much FUN the world can be when you look closely enough to notice the strange things God made — like almost-purple dragon slayers?

IS FOR...

Quad

Quad is a term that indicates "four." Some college campuses have a quad or quadrangle — which is a four-sided open-air court where students meet and greet one another as they cross the quad to get to the school buildings that surround it. Some prisons have a quad too! If you had QUADRAPHONIC sound, you could listen to music coming at you from FOUR speakers at the same time. If you were QUADRILINGUAL, you could speak in four languages — but not at the same time! What are your FOUR favorite things? Who are your four favorite people? Who are your four favorite heroes?

Quahog

Quahog is not some kind of hog — it's a clam! Isn't that a crazy name for a clam? Did you ever eat clam chowder or fried clams? Did you ever wonder about the expression "Happy as a clam"? Clams don't SEEM to be very happy, do they? Did you ever "clam up" and refuse to answer when someone asked you a question you didn't WANT to answer? Are you tired of all these question about clams? Well, clam up today and THINK about all the interesting creatures God made who LIVE in SHELLS — clams, turtles, oysters, and hundreds of others. If you have any shells, look at them closely and notice how each is a little bit or a whole lot different from one another — just like people's homes. Would YOU like to live in a big shell? If you could live ANYwhere, would it be by the sea?

OiNK OiNK

Quail

Quail is a little bird that is sometimes called a partridge or a bobwhite. But this word also has another meaning. When some people see danger coming or even think about it, they QUAIL or cower, shiver, and shrink from it. Did you ever see a quail? Did you ever quail with fear? Sometimes it's SMART to be afraid so you can get away from danger before it's too late. But sometimes you have to be brave and stand your ground. When someone tries to convince you to give up your values and do something you KNOW is wrong, you have to be brave enough to say NO. And THEN it's time to GET AWAY from that dangerous person!

Quartz

Quartz is a mineral that is often used in today's watches. Way back in 1880 a scientist discovered that if you cut quartz a certain way and passed electricity through it, the quartz would move back and forth at a constant rate. Many years later in the 1920s, clockmakers got the idea that they could use quartz this way to replace the machinery in a clock that went back and forth and made the sound of ticktock. Without the ticktock, they would have an accurate and SILENT clock. After the microchip was invented, it was possible to use this technique in small wrist watches, and now you can have accurate and QUIET time on your hands — or rather, on your wrist. Imagine what it must have been like before clocks and watches were invented. You would never know if you were going to be late or early! But it didn't matter — because nobody else knew either! NOW you have no excuse because there are clocks and watches everywhere — some that go ticktock and some that tell you the time without making a sound! Now that you KNOW what time it is, see if you can spend ten minutes of time without making a sound.

Question

Question is an inquiry, something you ask to get information or sometimes just to irritate! Some people seem to QUESTION everything! No matter what you say, they object and question whether you know what you're talking about. That can be irritating! But asking questions to get information, to learn more about a subject that interests you, can be an unquestionably wise thing to do. Do you ask a lot of questions? Why?

Quiddle

Quiddle is NOT a hot pan for cooking pancakes! A quiddle is a person who dawdles, wastes time, or does a job halfway instead of all the way. Why ANYONE would want to be a quiddle is a riddle. YOU would never want to be one, would you?

Quill

Quill is a large stiff feather from the wing or tail of a bird, and it was once used as a writing tool. Before people had ballpoint pens or fountain pens, they had ink. They would dip the quill into the ink and write a few words — and then the ink would dry up. So they would have to dip and write, dip and write, and it could take a VERY long time to write a letter. Today, you have ballpoint pens, typewriters, computers, and FAX machines so letters can whiz back and forth VERY quickly. Do you like to get letters or greeting cards? Well, so do other people! So why don't you send someone a letter or a card today?

AAH...

Quilt

Quilt is a bedcover that is made by stitching together lots of little pieces of material, and usually the pieces are all different colors and fabrics and designs. A quilt is like a family or a church — lots of individuals joined together to make something beautiful. Isn't that a warm happy thought — to be a unique, special, one-of-a-kind person and yet stitched together with lots of other one-of-a-kind persons to make the beautiful family of God?

Quirk

Quirk indicates something unexpected. It might be an unusual flourish in the way you sign your name OR a clever way of saying something old in a new way OR any unusual mannerism. Do you know anyone who has a quirk? Do YOU have any quirks? Which quirks do you think are good — and which ones are aggravating?

Quit

Quit is what you do when you finish what you're doing OR when you give up. It's good to know WHEN to quit. Some people refuse to quit when it's time to quit — like a tired but stubborn person who refuses to quit watching TV when it's time to quit and go to bed! Other people give up and quit too soon — like a lazy person who gets bored with a job that needs doing and gives up without getting the job done. One kind of person who hardly ever gives up is an inventor. Inventors just keep trying ONE MORE way to do something in a new and interesting way. There have been many great, useful inventions and many not so useful. Did you know that in 1950 a patent was issued for the invention of an automatic spaghetti-spinning fork? This is NOT an invention that might change the world! But many inventions HAVE changed the world — like the electric light, television, and the computer. When YOU have a good idea, don't give up on it. When you want to keep doing something but you KNOW it's time to stop, quit! Say a prayer every day to ask God to help you know when it's time to quit AND how to NOT be a quitter when it's time to keep trying!

Quiz

Quiz is a test, a number of questions you are asked to see how smart you are! This strange word for test probably comes from the Latin word *QUIS,* which means "who, which, what" — OR from another Latin word, *QUID,* which means "how, why." Do you like to ask questions? Do you like to take quizzes? Do you like to watch quiz shows on TV? Why don't you make up your OWN quiz today and then quiz somebody else? Make a list of some words from THIS dictionary OR from a regular dictionary. Memorize the meanings of the words and then quiz a friend — and see if your friend knows as much about words as YOU do. OR make a list of questions about things you DON'T know but would like to learn. Then ask someone else who WOULD know. A quiz can be fun — you can surprise someone else with what you know OR you can learn something new!

R IS FOR...

Rainbow

Rainbow is a lovely, hopeful, colorful sight that sometimes appears in the sky after a heavy rain or storm. It's caused by the reflection of the sun's rays in mists or sprays of raindrops. But it seems magical, mystical, and mysterious. Some people see it as God's sign to Noah after the great Flood, a sign that the world would never be destroyed by water again. Others see it as a sign of beauty and joy after the thunder and lightning of a scary storm. How do YOU see a rainbow? Watch for rainbows — not just in the sky but in yourself every day. Whenever something scary or stormy happens to you, be brave and pray and watch for God's rainbow of hope and joy that comes after the rain.

Red

Red is a bright exciting color that has MANY shades. A fire engine is red, but so is an apple — and they aren't quite the SAME shade of red. Some fire looks red and so does the inside of a watermelon, but they aren't the SAME red. There are also lots of different WORDS that can be used to describe red. Crimson, maroon, cardinal, and carmine are ALL reds, but each is a little bit different.

Just in the bird family there are the red-headed woodpecker, the scarlet tanager, the ruby-throated hummingbird, and the rose-breasted grosbeak. They all have red markings, but the red is a little different in each one. Wasn't God busy the day he decided to put the color red into the world? If you had to tell somebody about "red," how would you describe it?

Remedy

Remedy is a medicine or treatment used to cure or heal an illness or a problem. Through the years some people have TRIED some strange treatments looking for a remedy. Back in the seventeenth century, when there was a terrible illness known as the Black Plague, someone decided that maybe loud noises would BREAK UP THE AIR and get rid of the germs! They rang bells constantly and shot guns and cannons, but the terrible noise didn't cure the plague — and must have made the patients feel worse. Even in the twentieth century, people had the idea that you should put some garlic on a string and wear it around your neck so you wouldn't "catch" any kind of sickness. It probably worked because the garlic smelled so bad, people wouldn't get close enough to you for you to catch their germs! What do you think would be a good remedy — not for sickness but just for feeling bad and sad? How about a walk in the fresh air or doing push-ups or singing a song at the top of your voice? What cheers you up when you feel down? What do you do to cheer others up when THEY feel down?

Roller Skate

Roller skate is a skate with wheels that can make you whiz down the street — or fall on your nose. Some people who practice a lot can do all sorts of tricks on roller skates — spin and twirl and even dance! "Wheeled feet" are fun, but they can lead to tumbles. It would be nice if someone could invent a skate that would never LET you fall, but maybe it wouldn't be quite as exciting then. Maybe it would be nice to know exactly what is going to happen in the future, but that wouldn't be as exciting as wondering. God knows that humans love mystery and anticipation and suspense. That's why HE keeps the future secret while YOU wait and wonder.

Rouge

Rouge is a reddish cosmetic used to color the cheeks or the lips. You've probably seen many ladies who had lovely rosy cheeks, thanks to a bit of rouge — but did you know that MEN once wore rouge too? They did! In ancient Egypt, men even wore eye makeup — which you may have noticed if you've seen a picture of the golden mask of King Tut! And some of the makeup worn by women AND men in the past was poison! They didn't know that, of course, but many died because they had used makeup that contained lead, arsenic, or mercury! They wore makeup like rouge to make them look rosier and healthier, but instead it made them sick! Today, some people think if they drink too much alcohol or eat too much food or take drugs, it will make them feel better; but instead it just makes them sick. God expects you to take good care of your body — because he MADE that body for you!

Rubber

Rubber is an elastic waterproof material that can be used to make a variety of things — from tires for your car to an eraser for your pencil. It was first discovered in the sixteenth century when Spanish explorers in South America noticed Indians playing with a ball made from a substance they had never seen before. The ball was made from latex, the milky sap of tropical plants. Latex could be molded into any shape, but it got soft and sticky in high heat and hard and brittle when it was real cold. In 1839 a man named Charles Goodyear accidentally dropped a mixture of rubber and sulfur onto a hot stove and discovered VULCANIZED rubber, which could withstand heat or cold. Since then, synthetic rubber has been developed, and it is used along with the natural latex to make thousands of products from raincoats and boots to elastic bands and rubber stamps. And children still play with rubber balls just like the Indians did many years ago in South America. Who would ever dream that so many new things could be discovered and produced just from the sap of a plant? Nature is wonderful — and so are the people who are smart enough to put it to work for them and at the same time protect the environment.

S IS FOR...

Saddle

Saddle is a padded leather seat for a rider on a horse. Did YOU ever ride a horse and sit high in the saddle? Did you know a SADDLE FEATHER is a rooster's tail feather, SADDLE ROCK is a large oyster, and SADDLE SOAP is something you use to clean leather? Did you know that when someone has a problem or a hard job to do, they might say they've been "saddled" with a terrible burden? Were YOU ever saddled with a terrible burden? What did you do about it? Did you ask someone to help? They say "two heads are better than one," but since you have only ONE head, that must mean it's a good idea to put YOUR head together with somebody else's! So the next time you feel like a job is too hard for you to handle alone, don't be afraid to ask a friend to share your saddle!

GIDDYAP!

BURDEN

Safety Pin

Safety pin is a pin that is safe to use because it clips together so the sharp end of the pin can't reach out and stick someone! This is a great invention that we might not have if a man named Walter Hunt hadn't been broke. Back in 1849 Hunt owed another man fifteen dollars and couldn't pay it. The creditor told Hunt he would forget the fifteen dollars AND give him four hundred dollars for the rights to any kind of useful thing he could invent from a piece of wire. Hunt accepted the challenge. He spent three hours twisting wire and came up with the idea for the safety pin. Hunt got his four hundred dollars, his creditor got rich selling the new pin, and the rest of the world got a new way to get it all together without getting stuck! Have you ever invented anything? Have you ever been broke? Have you ever really looked at a safety pin? It's such a simple idea that you wonder why nobody ever thought of it before Mr. Hunt. But they didn't. Maybe there's an idea floating around today just waiting for YOU to be the FIRST to think of it. You think so?

Salt

Salt is something you sprinkle on food to give it more flavor. BUT did you know that out of every one hundred pounds of salt produced, only five pounds of it goes to the dinner table? The rest is used for different things such as tanning leather, making glass and soap, melting ice off sidewalks, and building roads. Salt was once VERY valuable, and people were VERY careful how they used it. Today, it's so plentiful that you take it for granted and never think about its value. It's one of those things that's just there — until you go on a picnic and have fresh tomatoes and NO salt because somebody forgot it! Do you ever take your family for granted because they're "just there"? Think about your family today. Think about how valuable they are!

Sidewalk

Sidewalk is a walkway for people who travel by foot! It's usually made of brick or concrete and MIGHT be on the side OR the front or the back or wherever somebody needs to walk. But one of the most important facts about a sidewalk is that ants LOVE to meet there. Almost any time you see a sidewalk, you can find some ants crawling across it! Nobody knows why — but some think it might be because people walking along often drop bits of candy or other food on sidewalks — and somehow the ants found that out! Ants are known to be very hard workers, but they aren't dumb. If people are going to drop food where it's easy to find, the ants might as well take advantage of it and enjoy their own "sidewalk cafe"! Are YOU ever guilty of dropping a candy wrapper, a soft-drink cup, or other trash as you walk along — instead of putting it neatly in a trash can? This would be a good day to resolve to always do YOUR part to keep your planet clean. And don't worry about the hungry ants looking for your candy wrapper — they'll find it in the trash can just as quickly as the sidewalk because ants are EVERYWHERE!

Silence

Silence is the absence of talk, sound, NOISE. A person can be silent. A room can be silent. But do you think a letter could be SILENT? Sure it could. There are many words in the English language with silent letters — letters that are included in the spelling but NOT in the pronunciation. For example, SUBTLE is pronounced suttle, INDICT is pronounced indite, YACHT is pronounced yat, and COLUMN is pronounced colum. How many other words can you remember that have SILENT letters? While you're thinking about that, also think about SILENCE. Have YOU ever tried it? Today, many people seem to be AFRAID of silence because they have to have a radio or television on ALL the time, so they never know what it would be like to experience the ABSENCE of noise! Why don't

YOU try it today? Go into a room by yourself, turn off all the noisy things, and be silent. Silence frees you to think, pray, or just rest without distractions. Some people think silence is as interesting as silent letters. What do you think?

Spectacle

Spectacle is a word used to describe something that is strange, dramatic, exciting, noteworthy — a sight you gotta see to believe! But a pair of "spectacles" are things you use to help your eyes see BETTER. Spectacles are eyeglasses! A man named Alessandro de Spina invented eyeglasses way back in 1285. They started out as pieces of special magnifying glass held together with a wire frame that would sit on your nose, so you could look out and see the spectacles in your neighborhood better! Today, "designer" eyeglasses are made with all kinds of fancy frames, in all colors, shapes, and sizes — and some of them are VERY spectacular! Imagine what it would be like if blind people could be given magic spectacles so they could see the world for the very FIRST time. EVERYTHING would be exciting — color, shadows, shapes, movement. Even a blade of grass, a bumblebee, a friend's face, would be a discovery! Close your eyes today and then open them and pretend YOU are seeing the world for the very FIRST time. Isn't the world wonderful?

Sphinx

Sphinx is a word that usually makes you think of Egypt because that's where tourists go to see the great Sphinx, a huge statue that has a face of a man and a body of a lion. Tradition tells us that the face on the great Sphinx of Giza was made to look like an Egyptian king named Khafre. This king was very rich and powerful and lived in the glittering golden splendor of a mysterious and fascinating ancient society. But you know what? He liked to play a game called "Hounds and Jackals"! Even famous kings must take "time out" sometimes. Would you like to go to Egypt to see the great Sphinx and the pyramids and the Nile River? What OTHER parts of God's world would you like to see? There are so many possibilities — deserts and rain forests, tropical jungles filled with colorful birds and slithering reptiles, and icy lands filled with icebergs and penguins. Think today about which part of the world you would like to explore. What about your OWN city or neighborhood? You might find it's a fascinating place too — if you pretend you're a hound or a jackal, lurking around corners, discovering a brand-new city! Try it — you might like it!

Sport

Sport is a diversion or pastime, something to do for fun and relaxation. It can also be a very competitive occupation for those who become professionals. But most people just enjoy either playing or watching some sport activity. A favorite sport might be baseball, football, basketball, hunting, fishing, bowling, soccer, or swimming. But did you know that in a prehistoric culture known as the Minoans, the most popular sport was bull-leaping? Daredevil athletes would somersault over the head of a charging bull! Does that sound like FUN to you? Well, what DOES sound like fun to you? What is YOUR favorite sport? Maybe you might like to play ball today or go swimming. If you do, or the NEXT time you do, thank God for making your muscles work so well so you can hit a ball or swim laps or just float in the water and give thanks that you won't ever have to somersault over a bull!

Squirrel

You've probably seen LOTS of squirrels: those furry little animals with the bushy tails that ALWAYS seem to be in a hurry. But did you know squirrels are color-blind? They see everything in black and white — just like an old black-and-white movie! Aren't you glad YOU see colors? And wasn't it nice of God to put so MANY wonderful colors in the world? Look around your world today and see how many colors you can count. What are your favorite colors? Which colors make you feel happy? If YOU could color the world in a new way, how would you color it? Would you make pink trees and blue snow? Orange grass and purple sunshine? Use your imagination and color today exciting!

Sugarplum

Sugarplum is a sweet treat — like a bonbon or maybe a compliment! Do you like "sweet treats" — candy, confections, compliments? Why, sure you do! Everyone NEEDS a little sweetness in life — but sweetness doesn't have to be cake and candy. It could be a great vacation, a silly joke, a new puppy, a trip to the zoo, a day at Grandma's house! What kind of "sugarplums" do YOU like best?

 # IS FOR...

Tablespoon

Tablespoon is NOT a spoon as big as a table! It IS a spoon to use to eat soup at the table or spoon up mashed potatoes at the table or maybe to dig a hole in the backyard to plant flowers by the picnic table. No, guess not. Digging with a tablespoon is usually frowned on as being a baaaaad idea. Did you know there is a spoon smaller than a tablespoon that is called a TEASPOON, and it can be used for lots of things besides stirring tea? Do YOU ever do any "stirring"? Have you ever stirred up a cake or stirred up trouble? Remember: Stirring up trouble can have a baaaaad result, but stirring up a cake can have a delicious result. So stir yourself up to have some fun today — but DON'T stir up any trouble!

Tablet

Tablet is a writing pad OR it can be a pill. And sometimes when you have to get out a tablet and write a note to say "I'm sorry" can be a job that's hard to swallow — just like a pill! If there's someone you've hurt or made angry, today would be a good day to get out that tablet and write that "I'm sorry" note. It may be hard to do, but remember — when you "take your medicine," you start to get well and feel much better!

Tack

Tack is a small, sharp-pointed nail, but TACKLE is something you use to catch a fish, and TACKY means shabby or in bad taste. See how you can "play" with words? You just add LE to tack and get tackle or add Y and get tacky. You can do this with LOTS of words. For example, you can add LE to pick and make pickle! Or you can add Y to bus and get busy! But this is just a beginning. You can add all sorts of letters to one word and get lots of brand-new words! You can turn a hat into a hatchet, a bat into a battery! For a fun game to play with your friends — or by yourself — make a list of words and then see who can make the MOST NEW words by adding extra letters to the old words! God must have had fun making the world — now YOU can have fun making words!

Tax

Tax is money you have to pay the government as a share of money you have earned or on property you own. Depending on where you live, you might pay income tax, real-estate tax, property tax, sales tax, and so on — and this can become a very "taxing" problem. Back in the days of the Romans, cemetery land was NOT taxed, so the famous poet Vergil came up with a burial "plot" to avoid paying tax on his home. He found a dead fly and held an elaborate FUNERAL FOR THE FLY! He invited friends to come and they all made speeches about the fly; then he buried the fly in his yard and claimed he did not have to pay taxes on his home because it was a cemetery! Most people HATE to pay taxes because they'd rather keep the money themselves, but they also realize that it's necessary for the people of any country to support their government — and taxes keep the government running. Say a prayer today for all the people who work for the government — especially the people who work in the tax department, collecting taxes. They have a HARD job!

Television

Television is something to watch! You also have to watch YOUR-SELF to be sure you don't waste time watching TOO MUCH television. Did you know there are as many TV sets in America as there are people in Japan? Did you know some people spend so much time watching TV that they don't have time to do anything else — like enjoy the sunshine outside, read an interesting book, play a game, join a club, or say a prayer? How much TV do YOU watch?

Thermos

Thermos is a hot and cold friend! It's nice to take along on a picnic in the summertime or to a football game on a cold winter afternoon. The thermos bottle — which can keep iced lemonade cold or hot chocolate hot — was really a happy accident! It was first invented in 1892 by Sir James Dewar as a scientific apparatus to keep heat away from the liquefied gas with which he was experimenting in the laboratory. His insulated container was later used by scientists to keep vaccines or serums at a stable temperature. But THEN a glassblower who made these containers for the scientists — Reinhold Burger — thought about how great it would be for campers, hunters, and picnickers to have a container to keep beverages hot or cold. He manufactured a small home "thermos bottle" and became rich and famous! Did you ever take a thermos on a picnic and enjoy a cool drink on a hot day? Aren't you glad Mr. Burger saw the opportunity to take one invention and turn it into another one? Always be ready to open the door when OPPORTUNITY knocks!

Time

Time is a special gift and every person — rich or poor, old or young, whatever race or religion or nationality — is given the same number of seconds, minutes, and hours in each day. But each one USES that time differently. And once used, time can never be brought back again. Time used in pouting, complaining, or being bored is wasted and gone forever. Time used in laughing, enjoying, doing worthwhile work, helping, or learning is gone forever too — but you have memories and accomplishments that you BOUGHT with that time. You didn't just throw it away and have nothing to show for it. How do you use the time YOU have been given? How will you use it in the future? Will you treasure and appreciate every precious minute? Maybe you should spend some time today thinking about TIME.

Trichomes

Trichomes are things that make springtime hairy as well as airy! Did you ever think of springtime as hairy? Well, it is! You see, trichomes are funny, fine little hairy sprouts that grow along stems and underneath leaves in the early spring. They can make a leaf as fuzzy as a cat's tongue! When the morning sun shines through the trees and bushes all "bearded" with these green "whiskers," the light seems to shimmer and float, making everything pale green, almost like the world is floating underwater. Did you ever notice that unusual pale green shimmer of springtime? Did you ever look at a leaf that is just sprouting or a flower just budding? They look so different when they're just beginning, when they're brand-new — the way babies look so different from first-graders and first-graders look different from teenagers and grownups. Plants and people grow in stages and ages — each different, each special, each good. Which age or stage do you think is the most fun, the most scary, the most exciting, the best?

Twinleaf

Twinleaf is a wildflower that was given the botanical name of "Jeffersonia diphylla" to honor Thomas Jefferson. (In case you've forgotten, Jefferson was the third president of the United States.) This pretty little white flower has an unusual leaf that is divided in half — each one looking a bit like a butterfly or maybe like an angel's wings. Thomas Jefferson grew these flowers in the beautiful garden at his home in Virginia. That garden and home — known as Monticello — have been preserved as historic "treasures" and are visited by many tourists every year. Today would be a good day to read a book about Jefferson and his many wild and wonderful inventions OR to plant some wildflowers in YOUR yard OR to take a walk and LOOK for wildflowers OR to thank God for all the wild and wonderful things he put on earth for you to enjoy.

Twist

As you might expect, this word can be "twisted" into many meanings! It can mean a kind of silk sewing thread OR the way you move when you dance OR the way you move your face when you MAKE A FACE! It can also mean a loaf of bread made of twisted dough or a kind of knot or a special way of throwing a baseball. What an interesting word! How many other meanings can you think of for this word? How many ways can you twist your face? Or your body? Or a piece of string or wire? There are so many "twists" in God's interesting world. Aren't you glad you live here?

Typewriter

Typewriter is a machine that prints nice-looking letters on paper, letters that are easier to read than SOME handwritten letters! The first typewriter that was invented by a man named Christopher Latham Sholes could only print ONE letter — the letter W! But he spent the next five years building dozens of typewriters and finally produced a practical model that would type ALL the letters of the alphabet. And if you've ever wondered why the KEYS on a typewriter are in a funny order — ASDF instead of ABCD — that's because Mr. Sholes arranged the letters so they wouldn't bang into one another and so the ones used MOST OFTEN would be within easy reach. His arrangement worked so well that keys on typewriters AND computers are still made that way today. Except in China! The Chinese use "characters" instead of letters, and some of their typewriters have fifty-seven hundred characters! Some of the keyboards are three feet wide and the fastest you can type on these machines is eleven words per minute. (On an alphabet typewriter, a good typist can type sixty to eighty words per minute.) Have YOU ever used a typewriter or a computer? Would you like to use a Chinese one? Type or write a letter to a very important person today — write a letter to yourself! And what should you tell yourself? Why, whatever you think you should know about yourself!

IS FOR...

Ultra

Ultra means beyond the ordinary, super, special. Life is ultra. Some people MAKE it ordinary by never noticing all the ultra things God put into life on earth — explosive thunderstorms, multicolored tropical birds that can TALK, multicolored tropical fish that GLOW in the dark, ugly green watermelons with delicious pink fruit inside, and unusual two-legged animals known as humans. ALL of those things are ultra — BEYOND the ordinary. So look around you today at all the ultra things in YOUR life. Take time to NOTICE all the excitement. Take advantage of all the possibilities. Never settle for the ordinary. God made this ultra world for you to SEE and appreciate. Don't disappoint him.

Umbrella

Umbrella is a funny-sounding name for a thing that looks like an upside-down saucer with a handle on it — which you hold over your head when it rains. Well! That sure sounds like a silly thing to do — standing out in the rain with an upside-down saucer over your head! But did you know the umbrella was first used thirty-four hundred years ago in Mesopotamia, a desert land where it almost NEVER rained? And that's how it got its funny name. The name *umbrella* comes from the Latin word *shade* because the FIRST umbrellas were used to protect Mesopotamians from the harsh desert SUN! The umbrella was used for years primarily to "shade" the person who carried it — and some rich people even EMPLOYED someone to carry an umbrella over them! Finally, Roman women got the idea of putting oil on their paper sunshades and using them in the rain. Since then, the umbrella has been used by everyone and anyone who is "too dumb to come in out of the rain." Actually, it's NOT dumb to enjoy the rain — a wonderful blessing that waters the grass, makes seeds grow, cleans the air, washes off house roofs, and gives trees a nice shower bath. What do YOU think about rain? Did you ever go out and walk in it on purpose WITHOUT an umbrella? Did you ever lift your face and feel the splatter of raindrops on your eyes and nose and cheeks? Why don't you try it sometime? You might think rain is a pain when you're on a picnic. But never disdain rain — because life WITHOUT it would be a real drain!

Ursiform

Ursiform is a word that Goldilocks should know about because it's an adjective that means "shaped like a bear"! When she saw Papa Bear, Mama Bear, and Baby Bear, do you guess she said, "My, how ursiform you are"? No, probably not. But did you know YOU can see bears in the sky at night? Two of the best-known groups of stars are known as Ursa Major and Ursa Minor — and they are sometimes called Great Bear and Little Bear. Go out tonight and look at the sky; see if you can count ALL the stars. If it's a cloudy night and there are only a few stars shining, you might be able to count all of them. But on a clear night only God can count ALL the stars.

Useful

Useful is a wonderful word because it means serviceable, helpful. Think today of what YOU could do to be "of service," to make a difference, to change the world, or to just make ONE person's life a little bit happier.

IS FOR...

Vacant

Vacant means empty, unused, nobody home! Do you ever FEEL vacant? Like nobody's home inside you? Well, that's the time to invite in a FRIEND! And you know who your BEST friend is, don't you? Yep, whenever you feel vacant or alone or lonely, invite God to come in and chat with you a spell. You never have to make an appointment with him. You don't have to bake cookies or have lemonade ready or make any kind of special plans. Whenever you feel like talking to somebody, all you have to do is sit down, get real quiet, and say, "Hi, God! Let's talk."

Vacuum Cleaner

Vacuum cleaner is a "dust removing" machine that uses suction to suck up all the dirt from a carpet or a corner or a floor or a footstool. You probably have a vacuum cleaner in your house BUT how would you like to have one as big as a refrigerator? That's how big the first one was! The first commercial vacuum cleaner was invented by a man named H. Cecil Booth in 1901. It was so big and heavy it took two men to operate it! Later, a smaller vacuum cleaner was manufactured that looked like a bagpipe attached to a breadbox! It LOOKED funny, but it not only helped clean up the country, it also improved health! The vacuum cleaner removed tons of germ-laden dust from theater seats, offices, shops, and homes. During World War I, it even stopped a "spotted fever" epidemic! The fever was killing Navy men quartered in a large building, and doctors thought the germs might be in the dusty air. So that big refrigerator-sized vacuum was brought in to clean the building, and TWENTY-SIX TRUCKLOADS of dust were hauled away and buried. That ended the epidemic. You probably never thought about how important a plain old vacuum cleaner could be! Maybe you should look around at all the other plain old ordinary things in your life and think how important they are. Life sure would be different if you didn't have a stove to cook food or a furnace to heat your home, an electric light to read by, a television or radio, a bicycle, an automobile, or even a can opener! Say a prayer today to thank God for putting such good ideas into the minds of inventors. Think about what YOU could do to invent something NEW in your life!

Variegated

Variegated means multicolored, streaked, or dappled with different colors — "livened up" by color or any kind of variety. A bunch of all-yellow flowers is very pretty, but a bunch of variegated flowers — all different colors — is bright and interesting because of the variety. Have you ever seen a sky that looked kind of ordinary UNTIL sunset? And THEN it became variegated with brilliant splashes of yellow, orange, pink, purple, and glittery gold? Could you imagine a sunset or a big garden of flowers or a whole world that was all ONE color? Even if it was beautiful, it would finally get boring, wouldn't it? Some PEOPLE want the world to always be the same, to never change, never be variegated. But God's world DOES change — seasons change from winter to summer, flowers go from bud to blossom, children grow up. Never be afraid of GOOD changes. Trust in God and ask him to help you value the variegated.

Vernal Equinox

Vernal equinox is a fancy-sounding name for the official beginning of spring in the Northern Hemisphere, a special moment when the day and the night are exactly the same length. There is another equinox — a time when day and night are equal — in the fall of the year, and it is called the AUTUMNAL EQUINOX. You have surely noticed how the days are short and it gets dark very early in the wintertime, but in the summertime you can stay outside much longer because it gets dark much later. The days and nights are not equal except at an equinox. You have probably also noticed that there are other things in life that are not always EQUAL. You might not be as rich or as tall or as smart as somebody else! But then somebody else might not be as rich or as tall or as smart as you! Life may not be equal, but it CAN be wonderful — if you look for the sunshine instead of the dark, the good instead of the bad, the blessings instead of the boo-boos.

Victim

A victim is someone who is hurt or "wronged" by another person. It's bad and sad to be a victim. But some people THINK they're victims when they're not! They have something called a "victim mentality." Every time something happens that does not please them, they think it is someone ELSE's fault or someone ELSE is picking on them. No matter what happens, they never take the blame but always blame somebody ELSE. Instead of working to overcome a problem, they just complain about it and feel very sorry for themselves. Beware of this trap. Whenever YOU feel wronged or hurt, talk it over and try to work it out. Learn the secret of happiness — "Only YOU can make YOU happy." With this secret — and God's help — you can become a victor instead of a victim!

Volunteer

Volunteer is what you do when you offer to do something you don't HAVE to do. But WHO would do something like that? Who would do EXTRA chores? Who would volunteer to help clean up after a party, work on a church committee, pick up toys in the middle of the floor, set the table for dinner, rake the leaves, cut the grass, help a sick neighbor by taking out the garbage or bringing in the morning newspaper? Who would ever offer to do these extra jobs? A volunteer would. Do you know any volunteers?

 # IS FOR WALL

Wall

Wall is a safeguard you put up to keep someone or something out OR in. It can be built of stone, brick, or plaster. A different kind of wall can be built of pride, hate, or fear. Did you ever hear of the GREAT WALL OF CHINA? It was built many, many years ago by the Chinese to keep OUT enemies and it winds along the countryside for almost two thousand MILES! Back in the Middle Ages many of the men who served as guards on the Great Wall spent their whole lives there. They were born there, grew up, married, died, and were buried — all at the same place. Of course, many people around the world know only the little village where they were born because they never have the opportunity to travel and see other towns or

cities. Do YOU like to travel and explore? Even if you NEVER take a vacation, you can travel by READING about other places and other people. Why don't you read about the Great Wall of China AND about the Berlin Wall of Germany and the Iron Curtain of Russia. Some countries have built walls to keep enemies out, but those same walls kept their own people IN — like prisoners. The same thing can happen when YOU build a wall around YOURSELF — a wall of pride or hate or fear. It can keep others out, but you can get lonely all alone, like a prisoner! So tear down your "walls" and let some friends in!

Warbler

Warbler is a bright-colored singing bird. These little songsters are often called the "butterflies of the bird world" because they are small, move fast, and have beautiful multicolored markings. In the summertime more than fifty kinds of warblers can be seen flitting through the sunshine and fluttering in the tree branches of North America BUT in the winter they vacation in the tropics. Some of the warblers have interesting names. There's the cerulean warbler, the Blackburnian warbler, the red-faced warbler (who is NOT embarrassed but DOES have a red face), and the prothonotary warbler. Did you know *prothonotary* can also mean a chief clerk of a court or a chief secretary of a church? Do you guess this bird has TWO careers — as a singer AND a clerk, with an office in a tree stump in a swamp somewhere? No, probably not — but it IS a funny idea, isn't it? Do YOU like to sing or warble in the shower? Sing a happy song today and give thanks for all the beautiful birds and butterflies that decorate our world. "This is the day the LORD has made; let us be glad and rejoice in it" (Psalm 118:24).

Water

Water is that wonderful, cool liquid that nobody can live without! It tastes so good when you're thirsty, and it tastes even better when it's used to make lemonade or root beer or your favorite cola. But do you know how many atoms are in one DROP of water? Well, if every person in the world joined together to COUNT the atoms in this ONE DROP, and all FIVE BILLION people counted one atom apiece every second, it would take them more than thirty thousand YEARS to finish counting! Can you IMAGINE how teeny-tiny each atom must be? Do YOU ever feel teeny-tiny and unimportant? If you do, remember that every single atom in that drop of water is important, and without even ONE, the drop of water would be different. If something so infinitesimal is important to God's creation of water, think how important YOU must be to God.

Wickiup

Wickiup is a kind of house. It's the name for a simple hut that was built by Indians of the southwestern United States. It was made with an oval-shape frame covered with a roof of grass or brushwood. Today, the word is used to describe any kind of simple hut. Wouldn't it be fun to spend a night in a wickiup? But then after a few days it would probably be even MORE fun to come home to a house with a refrigerator, a bathtub, and a TV set! Today, life is much easier

than it was when the Indians roamed the plains, living outdoors, hunting for wild game for each night's supper. Maybe that kind of life sounds like fun — and maybe it was. But it was also very hard. Give thanks for the EASY parts of your life and always ask God to help you with the hard parts. Pretend today that you are an Indian and imagine how it would feel to wander in the wilds and wake up in a wickiup.

Wish

Wish is a desire, a longing, a craving. You can wish upon a star! And if you were in a fairy tale, a fairy godmother might grant you three wishes for whatever your heart desired! What would YOU wish for if you had three magic wishes? Would you wish to be rich, famous, good-looking? How about wishing to be good? When you lead a good life, you're happy, and then you don't HAVE to wish — you can make your own dreams come true!

Wonky

Wonky is a British slang word that means shaky or tottery. Did YOU ever feel wonky? Sometimes if you've been sick in bed for a few days, the first day you get up and move around, you might feel wonky. Sometimes if you just haven't had enough sleep (like maybe when you slept in a wickiup and thought you heard wolves howling in the night?) and have to get up early, you feel wonky for the first few minutes. It can be a funny or even a scary feeling. Imagine how it must feel to be sick ALL the time and feel wonky every day. Say a prayer today for all the people who are sick at home or in hospitals. If you KNOW anyone who is sick, send that person a get-well card. (If you don't have one or can't buy one, you could always MAKE one. Often homemade cards are the very best!)

Work

Work is physical or mental labor that achieves a purpose. Work can be tiring, boring, and something you do NOT want to do. It can give you sore muscles (from working in the garden) or a befuddled brain (from trying to work out a budget or a math problem). But work is also rewarding! You work to get money to pay for something you need or want. You work to accomplish a goal or a dream, to get the knowledge for a career or a profession. Without workers there would be no homes, no food, no cars or candy bars, no baseball bats or silly hats, no planes, or trains or bathtub drains. Work can be wonderful IF you have the right attitude. What kind of attitude do YOU have about work? Do you hate it and try to get out of it or do you see it as a challenge, a way to achieve a goal? Think about work today. Or better yet, stop just THINKING and start DOING! Whatever work you have to do, get it finished — or at least get it started!

Wrangler

Wrangler is a name for someone who "rounds up" livestock on a ranch. OR it can mean someone who does some loud arguing. Have YOU ever been EITHER kind of wrangler? Have you ever tried to round up friends for a game or a party? Did you ever wrangle about who should be included and who should be left out? One kind of wrangling can be an important, constructive thing to do. Argumentative wrangling can be destructive. The next time you round up,

think about how YOU would feel if you were the one who got left out. The next time you start an argument, think about how it would feel to LOSE an argument. And right now, "podner," why don't you ask your folks if you can round up some friends for a western barbecue party? If you ask nicely, maybe you can WANGLE it! (Wangle is a slightly different word from wrangle because it means to get something through persuasion — INSTEAD of by arguing!)

Wriggle

Wriggle is a lot like wiggle and waggle. It means to twist and turn, jiggle and squirm. Did YOU ever do that? If you didn't, you must be the only person in the world who has learned how to NEVER ever get "antsy"! Sometimes whatever you're doing and wherever you are — in a classroom, a church, a theater, or just stretching out on your couch watching TV — you suddenly have the urge to MOVE. You might not even realize it, but all of a sudden you're twitching muscles, moving your body, rolling your head, or tapping your foot — and driving other people crazy! Why? Because wriggling is catching! As soon as someone sees YOU wriggle, they want to wiggle and waggle too! Do you feel like wriggling right now? Well, don't. See how long you can sit perfectly still without moving a muscle. It won't be easy! BUT it will be a good lesson in concentration. While you're sitting still, concentrate on how God made all your muscles and nerves and bones and brain work TOGETHER so you can run and reach and stretch and wriggle!

X IS FOR...

X

X is a letter of the alphabet that sometimes stands alone without any other letters. People say "X marks the spot!" because a simple X is often used on a map to indicate a special place — like the spot where a buried treasure is hidden or the spot where you're going on vacation! AND if you ever use Roman numerals, X equals ten. AND when a person doesn't know how to write his or her name, even legal documents can be signed by simply writing an X instead of a signature. AND people who DO know how to read and write sometimes end a love letter by adding an X to stand for a kiss! (When they put an X and an O, this stands for a kiss and a hug.) But did you know that X is also sometimes used to stand for Christ? It is. Do YOU always stand for Christ and his teachings? When someone tries to get you to do something wrong, do you ever explain that it would not be Christian to do that? It's not always easy to "stand for" Christ and his teachings, but it IS always right. So the next time someone who doesn't KNOW any better suggests you do something wrong, remember the X and what YOU stand for.

Xylocopa

Xylocopa is an odd-sounding word that means carpenter bee! And when would a bee be a carpenter? When he bores holes in wood. That's why these bees have such a strange name; it comes from the Greek words *XYLO* for wood and *COPA* for cut. Hmmm...wonder if these bees take woodworking classes in school? How would YOU like to be a carpenter OR a beekeeper? Both jobs are very worthwhile. Without carpenters there would be no nice houses to go to sleep in at night, and without beekeepers there would be no honey for breakfast in the morning. Think today about all the different jobs people have and what the world would be like if there was no one to do those jobs. What if there were no farmers, no bakers or grocery store owners, no garbage collectors, no electricians or plumbers, no TV repairers, no teachers, no mothers or fathers? What a sad world that would be. Which one of those jobs do you think you could do best? Which one would you LIKE to do?

Xylograph

Xylograph is an engraving on wood. Now MAYBE a xylocopa could make a xylograph, but it probably wouldn't be the kind you'd like to have in your home! Wood engravings are often very beautiful and very expensive. Have you ever seen a wood engraving? Maybe some day you'll see one in a museum or in a home or in an office. Wood engraving can be a fun hobby OR a very precise art. If you were a wood engraver, what kind of picture or design would you like to engrave — a tree, an animal, a winter scene, a sailing ship, a person? You might not be able to engrave a picture on wood today, but you COULD draw a picture. Get some paper and pens or paints and draw a picture of WHERE you would like to be or WHO you would like to be in the near future or maybe the far future. It's good to dream and imagine, hope and plan. And maybe some day you'll be where or who you dream of being.

Xylophone

Xylophone is a musical instrument that is made of wooden bars and played with wooden hammers. Maybe you've seen one or even played one. Another musical instrument is similar to this, but it's made of METAL bars and it's called a GLOCKENSPIEL! Both of these instruments have funny names but both are fun to play or to hear played. Some PEOPLE have funny names too, but you can't judge a person by a name or a house by its front door. You might be surprised to find what's inside the house OR the person. Do you know anyone who has a very unusual name? Some movie stars have strange names like Tex, Rex, Sissy, Sly, Petula, or Tallulah. If you were given a name that described your personality, what would your name be?

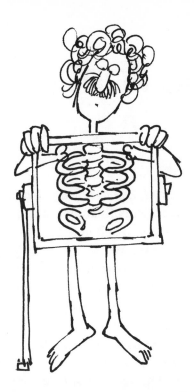

X-ray

X-ray sounds like something from a science-fiction story, but it's really something from a hospital! Whenever someone is sick, doctors first examine the person's OUTsides, and then they might use an x-ray machine to take a picture of the person's INsides. Did you ever go to a hospital as a patient OR as a visitor? It's nicer to be a visitor, isn't it? Then you can leave and go home instead of staying. But hospitals are wonderful places because that's where sick people can often get the kind of treatment to make them well again. And x-rays are wonderful too because they help doctors find out WHERE the problem is so they will know what to do to correct it. Don't you wish YOU had an x-ray machine so you could look inside heads to find out what people are thinking? Well, there's something even BETTER than an x-ray machine for that. It's called friendship. When you make a friend, you get to know each other so well, you KNOW what the other is thinking. Start today to make a NEW friend. You can never have enough friends!

Y IS FOR...

Yawn

Yawn is something that happens when you don't expect it and can't stop it! Your mouth suddenly flies open and anybody who's looking knows that you must be tired or bored. Why else would you be guilty of having a yawn on your face? Many, many years ago people were AFRAID of yawns. They thought if you opened your mouth that wide, your life breath might escape and you'd fall over dead! So when they felt a yawn coming on, they immediately put a hand over the mouth so the breath wouldn't escape. Today, polite people still put a hand over the mouth when they yawn — not because they're afraid but to keep other people from looking down their throats at their tonsils! Now we know yawns are not dangerous, but they ARE contagious. As soon as you see somebody else yawn, YOU want to yawn! And if you're in a room full of people, pretty soon

EVERYBODY wants to yawn. It's catching! What other things can you think of that are "catching"? Measles, the flu, a bad cold, or a bad mood? How about enthusiasm or Christianity? When you're with someone who is all grumpy, you sometimes start to feel grumpy too. And when you're with someone who is all excited and ENTHUSIASTIC about something (they say, "Let's go see that new movie!" or "Let's go on a picnic!" or "Let's make popcorn!"), you might start to feel interested and excited about the idea too! That's why even Christianity can be "catching"! Do YOU ever act so excited and enthusiastic about God's goodness and greatness and all God's wonderful creations and all the miracles and teachings of Jesus that other people get excited too — just from being with you? If you DO, you must have a lot of joy and gladness in your life. If you DON'T, maybe you should. Maybe you could start today.

Yo-yo

Yo-yo is a toy that began as a weapon! Back in the sixteenth century, Philippine hunters used a yo-yo that was made of large wooden disks wound with heavy twine. They would throw it at a wild animal and the twine would wrap around the animal and entrap it so the hunters could catch it. In the 1920s an American named Donald Duncan saw these weapons in use and got the idea to make a smaller version that could be used as a TOY — instead of a weapon! Do you ever FEEL like a yo-yo, going up and down, happy one day, sad or bored the next? Well, everybody has up days and down days. Enjoy the up days, and when a down day comes along, try to remember what you did on the up days to feel so good — and then do it again!

Yucatán

Yucatán is the name of a peninsula in Mexico. And do you know why it has this "yucky" sounding name? Well, they say that when the Spanish conquistadors first landed on the shores of this part of the world, the natives couldn't understand what they were saying. So the natives said to the Spanish, "Yucatán?" which meant "What? What are you saying?" But the Spanish thought they were telling them the name of the country. And the name stuck! It's so easy to mishear or misunderstand what someone else is saying — so always listen with BOTH ears. Sometimes you might think people are saying something yucky when they're just trying to understand what YOU are saying!

Yum

You can say yum or yum-yum or yummy! This is a word that SOUNDS like what it means — delicious! What kind of food do YOU think is yummy? What kind of school subjects do you think are yummy? Well, you need food for the BRAIN as well as for the body! And good brain food CAN be yummy and fun! Give your brain something delicious today. Read a book. Read a cereal box. Go to a library and discover something about some subject you didn't know about before. Call a smart friend and ask Smarty to TELL you something you didn't know before! And once you've stuffed yourself with smarts, think about what a delicious idea God had when he invented the human brain!

Z IS FOR...

Zabra

Zabra is NOT a zebra (which is, as you know, an animal that looks like a striped horse). A zabra was a small sailing vessel once used along the Spanish coast. Isn't it funny how so many things sound ALMOST alike but are SO different? You may look ALMOST like someone else (maybe you both have black hair and brown eyes and are the same height!) but you are SO different. Wasn't it nice of God to make each and every human being unique, special, and different from every other human being? Thank God today for making you just the way you are. Sometimes you may WISH you were different. You might wish to be taller, shorter, fatter, skinnier, have blue hair or orange eyes or long green toenails, BUT whatever you are NOW, you are special and loved. God loved you enough to make you in HIS image and to give you special talents. You may not think you HAVE talents but you DO! Make a list today of all your talents — the things that make you special. Are you good at building, cooking, painting, writing, spelling, helping? Do you have a talent for joy so you can make others giggle? Do you have a talent for caring so you can make others feel loved? You ARE talented and unique. You are the ONLY YOU in the whole world, and God loves you now — and will ALWAYS, always love you.

Zenith

Zenith is as high as you can get — the highest point, the peak. Do you ever aim for the highest? When you get something good, do you still want something better? When you get something expensive, do you wish for something that costs even more? Well, now let's talk about that. It's good to aim high — to want to BE something better, to want to act better or learn more or accomplish more. But to want to GET more? Maybe that's not the kind of zenith that makes people happy. Some people HAVE lots of expensive stuff and they still feel bad inside. Others have very little — maybe just enough to barely live — but they feel good inside and are happy and truly ENJOY life. It's not bad to have nice things, but THINGS never make people happy. So never aim ONLY for things. Aim instead to BE more, DO more, ENJOY more, and TRY more to help OTHERS enjoy life. That's happiness.

Zero

Zero is nothing, naught, of no value. They say that it's good to be well-rounded — to know a little bit about a lot of things, but they also say that if you are TOTALLY well-rounded, you are a zero! So decide today to SPECIALIZE in something! Find a hobby. Study a lot about one subject. Learn a skill. Discover how many kinds of shells there are in the world and what they look like. Study about art or apples, sculpture or salamanders, Indians or Indiana! Learn how to fly a kite, sew on a button, build a spaceship, or split an atom. Learning and doing make life exciting and fun. Don't be a zero. Seek, look, explore, discover, try something new, research something old. Enjoy life and all its possibilities!

Zigzag

Zigzag is a series of short sharp turns in alternate directions — a crisscross, a here and there, an up and down. You can zigzag down the street on a skateboard or zigzag across the lawn with the lawn mower (if you want a really FUNNY looking front yard) or zig when you should have zagged and get into LOTS of trouble! Think about the zigzags in your life. Some days you feel like dancing, the next day you feel like moping. One day life seems like a picnic, the next day it's the pits! Oh, well, just think how BORING it would be if life was just a straight line. Ask God today to help you learn how to laugh at the zigs and zags and ENJOY the excitement of the unexpected!

Zip

Zip is what you do with a zipper! So what's a zipper? It's that handy "slide fastener" that was invented by Whitcombe L. Judson more than a hundred years ago. The zipper was good news for most people but BAD news for people who made buttons. BEFORE the zipper, everybody had to buy LOTS of buttons to hold their clothes together. NOW you can zip up your raincoat and zip out into the storm, zip up your boots and zip out into the snow, zip up your jacket and zip out to the store or the movies or wherever. BEFORE you would have had to spend a lot of time buttoning up your raincoat, buttoning down your boots, and maybe buttoning your lip so you would stop complaining about how much time it took to get ready to zip out of the house. Do you think it might be a good idea to think about spending MORE time buttoning your lip? It's so EASY to blurt out an insult, a mean remark, a joke that makes fun of somebody else's weaknesses — so maybe you should try to do something HARD for a change! The next time you're tempted to say something "smart" that might make somebody else "smart" with hurt, remember that wonderful invention — the zipper — and zip your lip!

Zip-a-dee-do-dah

Zip-a-dee-do-dah is a funny fun phrase from a song. It's a good way to describe a happy feeling, a bright and sunshiny morning, or a new beginning. And maybe it's a good way to end a book. So here's to words, here's to discovery, here's to facts that are fun. Enjoy learning. Look up and out and in and all about. Get excited about what you see. Welcome wonderment! Then you'll have a zip-a-dee-do-dah day TODAY — and every day!

OTHER LIGUORI PRODUCTS

150 FUN FACTS FOUND IN THE BIBLE...
for kids of all ages
by Bernadette McCarver Snyder

This whimsically illustrated book offers 150 fantastically fun facts — full of surprises, secret messages, adventure, intrigue, and excitement...and they're all from the Bible! **$5.95**

365 FUN FACTS FOR CATHOLIC KIDS
by Bernadette McCarver Snyder

Start the day the fun way — with a fun fact, a daffy definition, a saintly surprise! There's one for each day of the year in this delightful book. Children will learn about heroes and heretics, papal bulls and bumblebees, lions and legends, and a whole lot more. **$5.95**

THE ABC's AUDIO/BOOK READ–ALONG PACKS

A special treat for kids — a fun, entertaining way to learn about our faith... Francine O'Connor's best-loved *ABC* books are now available as Read-along Packs. A lively reading of each book — enhanced by sound effects and music — is recorded on individual audio cassettes. Each cassette comes with a copy of the colorfully-illustrated companion book.

THE ABC's OF THE SACRAMENTS
...for children
(Read-along Pack — $9.95 / Book only — $2.95)
THE ABC's OF THE TEN COMMANDMENTS
...for children
(Read-along Pack — $9.95 / Book only — $2.95)
THE ABC's OF PRAYER
...for children
(Read-along Pack — $9.95 / Book only $2.95)